Conglomerates and the Media

Conglomerates and the Media

Patricia Aufderheide

Erik Barnouw

Richard M. Cohen

Thomas Frank

Todd Gitlin

David Lieberman

Mark Crispin Miller

Gene Roberts

Thomas Schatz

The New Press New York

Published in the United States by The New Press, New York
Distributed by W.W. Norton & Company, Inc., New York

The New Press was established in 1990 as a not-for-profit alternative
to the large, commercial publishing houses currently dominating the book
publishing industry. The New Press operates in the public interest
rather than for private gain, and is committed to publishing,
in innovative ways, works of educational, cultural, and community value
that might not normally be commercially viable.

Book design by BAD
Production management by Kim Waymer
Printed in the United States of America

9 8 7 6 5 4 3 2 1

Contents

PUBLISHER'S NOTE / **André Schiffrin** / 6

Introduction / **Todd Gitlin** / 7

New Look / **Erik Barnouw** / 15

The Corporate Takeover of News: Blunting the Sword / **Richard M. Cohen** / 31

Conglomerates and Newspapers / **Gene Roberts** / 61

The Return of the Hollywood Studio System / **Thomas Schatz** / 73

The Publishing Industry / **Mark Crispin Miller** / 107

Conglomerates, News, and Children / **David Lieberman** / 135

Telecommunications and the Public Interest / **Patricia Aufderheide** / 157

Liberation Marketing and the Culture Trust / **Thomas Frank** / 173

ABOUT THE CONTRIBUTORS / 191

Publisher's Note

This book came about through a unique collaboration between
The New Press and New York University's Departments of Culture
and Communications (Todd Gitlin), Education (Neil Postman),
and Journalism (Bill Serrin).

After much discussion, we all agreed that there was a great need
for a book that would look openly and critically at the impact
conglomerate ownership has had on the media. But it was equally
clear that no one expert could possibly cover all the changes taking
place. Accordingly, we came up with a plan to ask a group from
around the country, both academics and media critics, as well
as people who have themselves worked within the media, to come
to New York University and deliver a lecture around this question.

The lecture series took place in the fall of 1996, and drew large
audiences. The texts that follow are expanded versions of these
lectures, with one exception. Mark Crispin Miller has chosen to
substitute an essay on the state of American book publishing,
which appeared in a much shorter version in *The Nation*'s March
1997 issue devoted to book publishing.

We are all very grateful to our three co-organizers, as well as
to Ron Janoff, Larry Siegel, and Rick Hatala at New York University
for their assistance in organizing the lecture series.

André Schiffrin

INTRODUCTION

Today's media conglomerates have a grander scale than the trusts of the late nineteenth century, and more glamour. There is nothing secret about them. They are nothing if not brightly spotlit. The celebrity-choked press is enamored of the deals, awed by the size, complexity, and hypothetical synergy of the composite firms, which add up to what Thomas Frank aptly calls the culture trust. Murdoch/Disney/Time Warner/TCI sprawl through soft- and hardware, space and cable, wires and wireless, news and entertainment to bestride the earth. Stock analysts opine that the merger or acquisition of the week is a coup for one or another mogul. The burning question of the hour is: What occupies the mind, the walls, the menu, and the feet of Gerald Levin/Ted Turner/Rupert Murdoch/Michael Eisner/John Malone/Sumner Redstone/Barry Diller as this colossus contemplates the deal of deals? The journalism of the awe-filled room is usually too busy to ask what these immense mergers and acquisitions might mean for American—that is, world—culture. That is not the beat of the breathless chronicler. Nor are the prognosticators called to account for their previous financial projections, the ones that misfired.

Critics of the conglomeration juggernaut stress the danger that conglomerates will censor their wholly-owned news vehicles. In television, there are a few reported cases, enough to worry about, though the argument as usually presented is not rigorous enough. NBC in particular seems to have gone lightly reporting allegations against the parent company, General Electric. According to the television reporter Marc Gunther in the *American Journalism Review* (October 1995), a 1989 *Today* segment on defective bolts failed to mention GE, which used said bolts for nuclear reactors—mentioning GE only in a damage-controlling follow-up. A 1990 *Today* segment on consumer boycotts, Gunther adds, omitted any mention of a campaign against GE itself, and one guest has said that a producer cautioned him not to bring up the GE case. (NBC said this was the producer's say-so.)

In recent years, the creak emanating from the culture trust's news divisions is the sound of the industry bending over backwards to avoid the charge of taint. Since 1990, NBC has routinely covered GE scandals by name. On the *ABC News*, Peter Jennings has gone out of his way to cover criticisms of Disney. The first issue of Michael Kinsley's on-line Microsoft-owned *Slate* included a debate on whether Microsoft is a menace. It's a close question whether there's more to worry about from top-down censorship—an egregious case in point was corporate CBS's intervention to flatten down *Sixty Minutes'* treatment of tobacco—or from the long chill of a thousand microdecisions made by a thousand personnel about a thousand stories it would seem, well, more trouble than they're worth, to push too far. Self-censorship is probably the greatest danger, and it is rarely expressed; it leaves no smoking memos.

Since piper-payers have been tune-players since time immemorial, the fear of direct censorship is more than a bit naive, in fact. Just how rip-roaringly fearless were the networks in the good old days when Paley, Sarnoff, and other founding titans roamed the earth? William Randolph Hearst invoked sweetheart deals with theater chains to suppress *Citizen Kane*. The case against General Electric as such would be more impressive if critics compared NBC coverage of GE before its acquisition of RCA with coverage afterward. For that matter, does NBC cover GE differently than ABC, CBS, and CNN do? Did it before, when NBC belonged to RCA, a major military contractor among other things, not exactly the corner grocery store? Did CBS cover nuclear power questions more assiduously before Westinghouse, a nuclear power, purchased the company? We don't know.

What we do know is that conglomerates would seem to be setups for conflicts of interest between news and entertainment. When stockholders are being convinced that mergers are a good idea, these conflicts of interest go by the gaudy name of "synergy," and they are touted as a great good thing. *Time,* after all, devoted a cover story to Scott Turow, a Warner Books author, timed to the Warner Bros. release of the movie *Presumed Innocent. Time* found Turow more newsworthy than *Newsweek. Time* also featured a cover story on tornadoes the week that Warner opened its blockbuster *Twister.* On the other hand, *Time*'s coverage of the Bob Dole/William Bennett attack on gangsta rap did not fawn on the parent company, and was no more—or less—superficial than *Newsweek*'s. Movies and celebrities are the stuff of cover stories whoever the owner is. Here, too, the culture trust operates more subtly than one might fear.

Which is not to say that it operates less pervasively. Worrying is the closure of news that comes from closure of bureaus and miscellaneous cost-cutting. (The networks have precious few researchers as it is.) It stands to reason that reporters will also hesitate to take the risk of stepping on exposed toes. The larger and farther flung the enterprise, the more the toes and, therefore, the greater the risk for reporters. When, just after the deal was announced, Capital Cities/ABC's Thomas Murphy chided *Good Morning America's* Charley Gibson for doubting how glorious it would be to work for the Disney "family," what was he signaling?

It comes as no surprise that the culture trust devotes little energy to analyzing itself. In 1996, television and newspapers alike showed precious little interest in the momentous telecommunications legislation that Congress passed and the President signed. Among its myriad provisions, the new law permitted the cable companies to compete in the telephone business, eased restrictions on the number of radio or television stations a single company could own, and lengthened broadcast license periods to eight years. One fragment of the new law of the land concerned the famous V-chip, V for violence or veto, that little built-in device designed to help parents reclaim some control over the so-called culture in which their children are daily marinated. The president derived much satisfaction from outflanking then Senate Majority Leader Bob Dole on the media morality front and jawboning media executives into sounding a couple of cheers for the V-chip.

According to the Nexis data–base, while major newspapers mentioned the V-chip 1,391 times during the first six months of 1996, they mentioned broadcast license terms *not once*. Granted, license renewals are pretty, well, *heavy* stuff for today's newspapers. As younger people chuck all that messy print and divert themselves in droves, media moguls blame their losses on TV and resolve to make their papers look even more like TV screens. Take Knight-Ridder chairman Tony Ridder, whose chain ranks second in circulation nationally. In 1995, Knight-Ridder company profits were estimated at 9.9 percent, compared to winner Gannett's 20.8 percent and the industry average of 13 to 14. Whereupon Chairman Ridder, known to some of his employees as "Darth," announced plans to cut news staff at his *Miami Herald* by 9 percent. Unlikely that this plan would meet much resistance from *Herald* executive editor Doug Clifton, who said publicly that he'd not "really 'read' a Bosnia story in two years."

How bad is the merger news? In the case of books, the conglomerates clearly dumb down their tastes. They demand higher sales thresholds than before, extract high overhead charges, overpay for potential best-sellers, and in many ways crowd out the space for so-called "midlist" books. In the case of movies, they stuff the theaters with soulless blockbusters. In the case of newspapers, the hard evidence is equally clear: conglomerates are brisker dumbers-down than single-ownership organs. They care more about profits. The more newspapers in a chain, the fewer the column inches devoted to news, the shorter the articles, and the higher the proportion that goes to soft stuff. This does not mean that the articles are necessarily skewed to the right of where they would otherwise be. Those who think that the reason Americans are conservative today is that they're brainwashed by conglomerates have yet to reckon with the fact that some of the greatest progressive change in twentieth-century America took place in the 1930s, when newspapers were overwhelmingly, outspokenly right wing.

The worst hasn't happened (yet), but then again, some critics have been looking for dangers in the wrong dystopian places. Big Brother isn't looming, Brave New World is. The point is not that the media were once fearless and are suddenly in danger of becoming fearful; or that entertainment was once brilliant and is suddenly in danger of dumbing down. (Network television in the fabled '60s, for example, was largely brain-dead.) No one who worries about trusts proposes a return to the narrow pipeline of yesteryear. The question is: What brand of diversity will the titans indulge? Most likely, immense varieties of segmented entertainment. Serious art is at a premium, and ideas are scarce unless they can be channeled into "You're-a-jerk-no-*you're*-a-jerk" McLaughlin-type cartoons. While so-called conservatives in full campaign voice fulminate in behalf of the virtue of virtue, in office, they preside over the deregulation chorus, celebrating purely and simply the virtue of "the market," that contemporary God to which prayer is daily delivered. It suits the parties in power to collect impressive sums from the titans while proclaiming the virtues of self-regulation. Follow the money from media and you see a lot of it flowing into the punchbowls of both political parties. The point is that the changes now in progress are largely irreversible, potentially consequential, and they are being left to marketeers whose commitment to the public domain is dubious. The fact of diversification is offered up as proof that competition delivers all the goods anyone could possibly want.

Now, it is true that two phenomena have grown simultaneously in America's media. One is conglomeration. The other is segmentation. Demographic slices are the targets in cable TV, radio, magazines. If choice is the champion goal, then the more choice the better; and clearly Manhattan's Time Warner Cable, with 76 channels, cannot be worse for consumers than the precable array of seven VHF channels. Can it?

Not in the obvious sense, although the proprietors of cable TV have a lock on access. These effective monopolies permit and deny access just as they choose. Accountability is not their game. Giving preferences to their corporate partners is. Catering to high-spending demographics is. But the standard of comparison ought not to be the impoverished past. The relevant question is about democratic potential. Surely, Congress and the press might spare 10 percent of the time, money, and energy they have devoted to the Whitewater scandals to the rather more momentous question of the impact of centralized power on the nation's sluggish flow of ideas.

Instead, trusts with an immense capacity for overbearing power are being merged and acquired into existence as if there were nothing at stake but stock values. Today's deals may weigh on the culture for decades. The potential for harm is at least as impressive as the potential for good. If the country believed in the countervailing authority of the government, the recourse would be obvious: Time for the sheriff to step in and rumble in his gravelly voice: *Not so fast.* But the sheriff has been disarmed—at least politically. It suits the parties in power to collect impressive sums from the titans while proclaiming the virtues of self-regulation. If the issue were street crime, conservatives would be crying out against such an abject surrender.

America is the only nation, great or otherwise, that charges its political candidates for the right to use the principal means of communication. Meanwhile, television battens on federal largesse. The licenses which are the indispensable foundation of network spoils are cheaper than gold-mining rights on federal land in Wyoming. Thus is the circle of meretriciousness seamless. Corporate media buy politicians who depend on them, and, as for regulation, let the public eat V-chips. Intense and informed discussion of these matters is long overdue.

Toward this end, the articles in this volume make a real contribution. They were the brain children of André Schiffrin, director of The New Press, and began as lectures sponsored by the Departments of Culture and Communication, and of Journalism, at New York University, during the fall of 1996. From within and without the industry, they touch on central historical, political, legal, and cultural aspects of the conglomerates and their consequences. They raise the quality of the discussion, remind us of democratic hopes, and would shame politicians and moguls alike—if these barons of popular culture were not shameless.

This introduction draws from material previously published in the *Media Studies Journal* and the *New York Observer*.

Erik Barnouw

NEW LOOK

Traveling on a once familiar road, and seeing how unfamiliar it has become, can be fascinating but slightly jolting. I've been experiencing that while approaching the task assigned to provide "the long view on American radio and television." My first thought was, "That should be easy enough. I've been there, done that." But not quite.

In the light of a new day, nothing looks quite the same. Familiar details take on new meanings. A new look is clearly needed.

I want to begin, this time, with a short poem, one that seems to me oddly appropriate. Actually, it isn't a poem at all. What it is, is the incorporation certificate of the American Telephone and Telegraph Company. The date is 1885. The document has such infectious cadences, and such a visionary quality, that I began to think of it as a brief epic poem. It goes like this: AT&T proposes to

> connect every city, town and place in New York State with one or more points in every other city, town, and place in said state—and in each and every other of the United States—and in Canada and Mexico—and each and every other of such cities, towns, and places is to be connected with each and every other city, town, or place in such states and countries— and also, by cable and other appropriate means—with the rest of the known world—as may hereafter become necessary or desirable in conducting the business of this association.[1]

This seems to me a grand document. It has a sweep, a confidence—a chutzpah, if you like—that is dazzling. What I've included is just one sentence. At its start, we were in New York, back in 1885. By the time the sentence ended, we were in a very different world—a worldwide-web-world—with global conglomerates doing what was necessary or desirable for business. In short, the world we now enter and contemplate.

I thought it might be interesting, perhaps useful, to recall some of the transitions, the turning points, that took place between the beginning and end of that sentence. Some foreshadowed things to come. Some involved bitter disputes.

Note that AT&T, as it prepared to interconnect humanity, wasn't thinking just of wires and cables, but also of "other means" that might turn up. In the 1880s, the scientific world was abuzz with talk of Hertzian waves—radio waves—and how they might be used to send messages through space. And it was talking about the odd Nipkow disc, the rapidly rotating disc that would seemingly make it possible to send pictures—still or moving—by wire or through space. Details had to be worked out, but AT&T was clearly alert to any "other means" that might assist its agenda.

A transition I find especially fascinating began in 1920. That year, when the Commerce Department began to offer *broadcasting* licenses on the heels of the KDKA triumph, it set off a stampede. By July 1922, over four hundred stations were on the air, with more on the way. Many were prewar amateur rigs upgraded for the new era—transformed into broadcasting *stations*. Many diverse interests were brought into play. More than seventy of the stations, the largest group, were launched by universities or colleges, inspired by visions of a new era in adult education. Others were started by newspapers, hotels, manufacturers, department stores, religious groups, and others. All saw in broadcasting an extension of whatever they were already doing; in other words, all had some promotional aspect. But none, at this point, sold time for advertising. In fact, the mere suggestion of doing so could bring rebuke. Commerce Secretary Herbert

Hoover, presiding proudly over this extraordinary eruption, said it was "inconceivable that we should allow so great an opportunity for service to be drowned in advertising chatter." It was indeed an idealistic moment. Hoover, by the way, credited the eruption to "the genius of the American boy."[2]

During 1922, the fever generated an orgy of prophecy, not unlike other such orgies. The Doubleday company launched a new magazine, *Radio Broadcast*, to chronicle the coming age. Broadcasting, said the magazine in its first issue

> will elicit a new national loyalty and produce a more contented citizenry...

> the government will be a living thing to its citizens instead of an abstract and unseen force...

> elected representatives will not be able to evade their responsibilities to those who put them in office...

> at last we may have covenants literally openly arrived at...

> the people's university of the air will have a greater student body than all our universities put together.[3]

Also in 1922, a former secretary of the navy, Josephus Daniels, dedicating a station in North Carolina, said: "Nobody now fears that a Japanese fleet could deal an unexpected blow on our Pacific possessions.... Radio makes surprises impossible."[4]

(All this suggests that a pundit's lot is not, in the long run, a happy one—which may be a good thing for all of us to keep in mind.)

The exhilaration of 1922 brought more and more stations to the air, and Hoover began to worry—for good reason. The licenses had all been issued under a radio law of 1912, a very ambiguous document. Hoover, studying it, was sure he had the right to issue licenses, but probably not to refuse them—not to U.S. citizens, anyway. And the law did not explicitly define regulatory powers. Hoover kept urging Congress to pass a new law to clarify all this, but the uncertainties of the future made this difficult and led to endless congressional debate, while still more stations came on the air. Hoover invited radio leaders, including those from Westinghouse, AT&T, and General Electric—the titans of the era—to Washington to advise him about the chaos. They urged him strongly to ignore his doubts about the law, to issue firm regulations, and establish order. They promised to support him. Hoover thought it might be the first time an American industry had begged to be regulated.[5]

About this time AT&T announced a plan of its own, which it said would solve many problems. The company would start a new, specialized kind of broadcasting station, which it compared to a telephone booth. Just as one could step into an AT&T phone booth and, for a small coin, talk with a friend across town or in another town, so one would be able to enter an AT&T radio station and, for a fee, address the world at large. AT&T said it would soon have such a station on the air in New York, followed by stations in other cities.

The company did not use the word "advertising" but it seemed to mean that and protests came. The magazine *Radio Dealer* assailed AT&T's "mercenary advertising purposes." *Printers Ink* said it would prove "positively offensive." But AT&T stuck to its guns. It got its New York station on the air by mid-1922. On August 28, the first advertiser entered the phone booth. This pioneer was the Queensboro Corporation, which wished to promote the sale of apartments in a Jackson Heights cooperative. In other words, it was selling condos. To this end, it invested $50 in a ten-minute afternoon pitch. This was such a historic moment that I want to read you at least part of it. The spokesman said:

> I wish to thank those within sound of my voice for the broadcasting opportunity afforded me to urge this vast radio audience to seek the recreation, and the daily comfort, of the home removed from the congested part of the city, right at the boundaries of God's great outdoors.... The cry of the heart is for more living room, more chance to unfold, more opportunity to get near the Mother Earth, to play, to romp, to plant, and to dig. Let me enjoin upon you as you value your

health and your hopes and your home happiness, get away from the solid masses of brick, where the meager opening admitting a slant of sunlight is mockingly called a light shaft, and where children grow up starved for a run over a patch of grass and the sight of a tree. Apartments in congested parts of the city have proven failures. The word neighbor is an expression of peculiar irony—a daily joke.... The fact is, however, that apartment homes on the tenant-ownership plan can be secured by..."[6]

And so on. It will not surprise you that the American dream—and family values—was what this event was "all about." It was "all about" other things, too. For example, it was about a new push to suburbia, spearheaded by the automobile and the radio. Radio, it was said, had removed the last obstacle to living in the country. Automobile and radio had ended the sense of isolation associated with country living. The event was about other things besides—such as, a turning point in the history of advertising. The Queensboro Corporation broadcast four more $50 afternoon talks and an evening talk at $100. Apartment sales, to a value far exceeding these investments, apparently resulted. Others were now ready to enter the phone booth: American Express, Tidewater Oil, Goodrich, also a beauty product, Mineralava, which presented Mary Pickford talking about "How I Make Up For the Movies." Photographs of Mary were offered to listeners writing in, and these provided some demographic data on the audience. AT&T handled these developments shrewdly. Though some of the advertisers had approached the station directly, AT&T paid a 15 percent commission to each company's advertising agency, matching commissions paid by print media. This gave the agencies a strong reason for getting into the game. In business terms, radio had joined "the media."

Inevitably, this brought more stations to the air, many of them time-selling stations, which soon began to be linked by AT&T with other "commercial" stations, as they came to be known—all able to receive, via AT&T lines, treasures like sport events described in action, which became powerful magnets for listeners and sponsors.

Broadcasting had been described in 1922 as a unique opportunity for service. By 1924, more thought of it as a likely chance for a killing. So the rush to the air intensified, as did the spectrum chaos. By 1924, Hoover, still waiting for Congress to pass a new law, felt the chaos had become intolerable. He decided to act as the advisers had urged. New requests for licenses began to be handled with a form letter, saying "all available wavelengths" were now in use, so the requests could not be granted. Meanwhile, Hoover began a drastic realignment of existing stations, dividing them into categories. Most, including almost all educational stations, were dubbed "local" stations. They would be on the same wavelength as a host of other local stations, so had to be limited in power—100 watts or less—to avoid interference. Then there were "regional" stations, on a different wavelength, which they shared with other regional stations, all distant enough to permit more power to be used. Finally there were "clear-channel" stations, free of interference over most of the country, and therefore allowed maximum power, eventually, in many cases, 50,000 watts or even more. AT&T's stations, and those of General Electric and Westinghouse, which all "went commercial," were in this favored group. Nonprofit broadcasters noted that Hoover had created a hierarchy of stations, and that they, themselves, were at the bottom of it. Bitterness developed.

Why had Hoover done this? He had apparently adopted a rationale used by AT&T in promoting its plan. All those other stations, AT&T argued—educational or religious or whatever—were "special-interest stations", whereas an AT&T station was "for everybody." Anyone could buy time on AT&T stations, so they would be the epitome of democracy. They served the "*public* interest."[7] AT&T also argued that those it called "special interests," such as education, didn't really need stations; they could buy time on AT&T stations, save money, and help clear the chaos. It would not be the first or last time that creative use of language played a part in media struggles. When the Federal Radio Commission later took over the licensing function under the Radio Act of 1927, it used the same rationale, as it, too, began moving stations around the dial. The *Harvard Business Review*, in a detailed study of the commission, concluded: "While talking in terms of the public interest, convenience, and necessity, the commission actually chose to further the ends of the commercial broadcasters. They form the substantive content of public interest as interpreted by the commission."[8]

I probably need not remind you that all this was during the administration of Calvin Coolidge, who assured us: "The chief business of the American people is business."

With licensing halted, would-be broadcasters felt frustrated but found there was another way to get a channel. You could buy one. A commercial applicant sometimes found a discouraged nonprofit ready to give up, at a price, and then found that the Commerce Department was ready to bless a transfer—channel and all. This seemed at odds with the law, which gave a licensee the use, not the ownership, of a channel. So how could he sell the channel along with his equipment? However, the department took the view, as its spokesman explained to a Senate committee, that "the license ran to the apparatus." With this green light, a traffic in licenses quickly developed.[9] A commercial applicant found that it could petition the commission for the right to take over, "in the public interest," a channel in use by someone else, presumably in a less worthy manner. The commission would set a "comparative hearing," and the nonprofit would have to send a lawyer to Washington to defend its channel, perhaps losing in the process. Nonprofits grew increasingly wary. Meanwhile, their presence in the spectrum seemed to be resented. Without profit to anyone, they were sitting on channels that could earn someone a small fortune. Via purchase or pressure, many nonprofits were now to be edged off the dial. Much effort and money went into this.

The Federal Radio Commission was a body drawn largely from businessmen. Taking office in 1927, it found 712 stations on the air and decided that was too many. Ninety of them were operated by educators. The commission began a grand new shuffle, from which most educational stations emerged with part-time licenses, many confined to daytime hours, which were generally considered of lesser value for adult education. In dismay or disgust, eight educational stations left the air in 1927, twenty-three in 1928, thirteen in 1929. A few years later, only about two dozen hung on.

There are several ways to recap the story of broadcasting in the 1920s. One is to say that it began in euphoria with visions of an age of enlightenment, but ended with the rout of the educators. The educators eventually bounced back, but that is a later story.

Another way to describe it—the industry version—is that during this time the American people decided, in their democratic wisdom, that the nation should have a broadcasting system based on advertising. This version isn't quite accurate, though often repeated. In fact, there never was a time when the people's representatives in Congress were asked to decide this issue. Perhaps it seemed too risky to put it to a vote. Anyway, it was not decided in that manner, but via business decisions never effectively challenged.

Still another way to describe it is to say that the traffic in licenses, which made licensing incidental to buying and selling equipment, began during these years, with the result that regulators virtually handed control of the spectrum to private interests. This traffic—with occasional, gallant resistance by individual commissioners—has thrived ever since, bringing a constant escalation in prices, and excluding from the game all but the very well-to-do.[10] This has made our industry's structure increasingly undemocratic, giving us such recent phenomena as the transfer of NBC, along with RCA and all their licenses, to General Electric. Thus, one of our major news sources became the property of a company selling military equipment, collaborating in the planning of Star Wars, and marketing nuclear plants at home and abroad. Every NBC newsman went onto a payroll controlled by GE, and was kept aware of it.[11] From a standpoint of public policy, it is hard to think of a sorrier linkage.

But perhaps the most relevant way to describe the twenties is to say that the struggle between private and public interests for the soul of American broadcasting was joined then and has remained a central theme in media annals— of increasing significance as we, once more, move into a new "gee whiz" era.

Reviewing the long saga, I have been amazed at the antagonism, the truculence, that has often marked the struggle. In the early thirties, educators, dismayed by the commercial takeover, began to press for special channels earmarked for education. The new magazine *Broadcasting*, which generally reflected commercial interests, responded as follows: "Education has been used as a cloak to cover many sins in this country and it may be that we shall be sentimental enough to permit the educational lobby to get away with this grab. But anyone who thinks it will increase the pleasure of listening to the radio is a sap."[12] A federal radio commissioner, Harold LaFount, when asked his opinion, said: "What has education contributed to radio? Not one thing. What has commercialism contributed? Everything— the life blood of the industry."

The other side had answers to all this. As radio sponsors multiplied and filled the air with commercials and merchandising schemes, the influential Senator Burton K. Wheeler of Montana compared it to "a pawnshop." A dean of the University of Illinois called it "a sickness in the national culture." And the inventor Lee de Forest, often called "the father of radio", cried out in dismay: "What have you gentlemen done with my child?... You have made of him a laughing stock to intelligence, surely a stench in the nostrils of the gods of the ionosphere."[13]

In 1934, Senator Wagner of New York, who had similar feelings, proposed a measure by which all existing licenses would be voided to prepare for a new deal in the spectrum, in which a fourth of all assignments would go to nonprofits, and these would be equal in power to commercial stations. This measure escaped passage by a narrow margin, but the pressure helped to produce a kind of radio renaissance in the late 1930s. Broadcasters applying for license renewals were asked to list hours they had devoted to public services. This period gave us the famous CBS *Workshop* series, marked "not for sale" in CBS rate cards, and offering such works as MacLeish's *Fall of the City*. The period also gave us forums like *America's Town Meeting of the Air*, Edward R. Murrow's *World News Roundups*, Orson Welles and his *Mercury Theater on the Air*, and works of Norman

Corwin, unofficial poet laureate of the war years—all introduced as nonprofit items. Radio's approval rating soared during these years.

In 1952, as television began its first great boom, the idea of reserved channels for education took hold. Congress legislated the needed channels, but not the necessary funds. So there was delay as educators tackled the fund-raising problem. Meanwhile commercial applicants ceaselessly pressured the FCC to release the channels for commercial use. *Broadcasting* magazine, backing them, warned: "One day the FCC must take another look at the Communications Act in relation to these socialistic reservations."[14]

When the FCC ignored this advice, the magazine predicted that there would soon be a cleanout at the commission, beginning with a probe by Senator Joseph R. McCarthy of Wisconsin. The magazine considered the members of the FCC "stooges to the communists."

Our broadcasting history seems to have been accompanied, through months and years, by just this kind of altercation, or rhubarb, or brouhaha, or dialogue if you like. It should not surprise us that the industry emerging from it shows similar ingredients, all longtime elements in our culture. And it should not surprise us that its programming now shows similar strands, from the sourest reactionism to the sunniest progressivism. As in many a family, my wife and I often start an evening by saying, "I guess there's nothing on television." But, in truth, we often find something—on television and on radio. I might summarize by saying, we tend to look on current fare as still Newton Minow's vast wasteland, yet across it we find oases, many of which we treasure. To carry confession still further, in summer we try to have a swim every afternoon. We do this ten miles away, at an old stone schoolhouse I bought years ago, where one of my daughters now lives, and which we equipped with a swimming pool. On the way there, we listen to *Fresh Air*, in which Terry Gross's lucid interviews, the finest on the air, provide an update to anyone's education. On the way back we tune to *All Things Considered*, probably the most enlightening journalism on the air. On Saturdays, we go on from there to listen to Garrison Keillor, who seems to have reinvented radio, and is also a worthy successor to Mark Twain. As you can see, we gravitate toward the public media, yet we also find our oases on cable and network. We treasure C-SPAN. We honor *Sixty Minutes* and its astute, responsible whistle-blowing. And each year the networks seem to give birth to one or two sitcom series that rise above formula and tell us something of the human condition— series like *M*A*S*H*, or *All in The Family*, or *Roseanne*. Such series seem worth keeping an eye on. So we keep surfing the channels, occasionally marveling at flashes of genius emerging from unexpected corners. But, mostly, we watch public television which, in spite of all the obstacles thrown in its path, and the venom sometimes leveled at it, has survived, and somehow turned into what it was meant to be: "a civilized voice in a civilized community." The documentary genre, a special interest of mine, has tended to degenerate under commercial auspices but on public television has achieved some of its finest hours. I would hate to have missed the masterly presidential biographies by David Grubin on *The American Experience*, or the recent brilliant series on the first world war, titled *The Great War*, or various items on *Frontline, Nova, P.O.V.* and other PBS series. We are grateful for *Masterpiece Theatre*. And isn't it nice that our noncommercial television, which has no sure source of funds, can turn to the BBC, which does have, to acquire many memorable programs.

Like many interesting eras, ours has seen the accumulation of great fortunes. In ours, as in others, some of this has been channeled into matters to benefit society, including education and the arts. Great fortunes are ascribed variously to shrewdness, hard work, good luck, talent, and greed. I have been less concerned with how wealth was amassed than with the use eventually made of it. And when I see the surplus cash of a General Motors making its way, via a prod from tax incentives, to the workshop of a Ken Burns, to metamorphose into such rare, deeply moving projects as *The Civil War* and *The West*, I rejoice, and almost find myself saying, "We need the greed." Yes, perhaps we need the greed, but also the vision and organizing genius of a Ken Burns, and also the tax incentives. I was glad to note, in the recent campaign, President Clinton's frequent references to such targeted incentives. Surely, they are essentials in the total mix. They serve as a valuable bridge between public and private interests.

I gather there are still those who would wipe out, or "nuke," as the saying goes—or privatize, which may mean the same thing—such public creations as National Public Radio and Public Television, along with Headstart and Americorps and other life-enriching services. The late elections suggest that the larger public does not share the urge to self-mutilation.

There can be no doubt that our system of sponsored broadcasting has brought rich funds to our industry, giving it power and a global reach. We have, at the same time, paid a price for this. The frenetic selling has sold many things, including salesmanship. I am told that in kindergarten today, nothing motivates a child more than the chance to stand up and "do a commercial." In the 1980s, the Screen Actors Guild revealed that its members were earning more from commercials than from theatrical films, and television films, and all other kinds of films combined. This seemed to me a depressing statistic. I assume it has furthered our obsession with products, which are constantly offered as the key to success in business, romance, community relations, and the well-being of society. The American people, once addicted to frugality, now seem obsessed with their role as consumers. Descartes said: "I think, therefore I am." We have made it: "I buy, therefore I am."

A special price has been paid in several areas of society. One concerns children. Broadcasters early learned that salesmanship addressed to children can exert profitable leverage on the parents, the buyers. This was a favorite talking point in the early promotion of radio as an advertising medium, as in a famous trade advertisement of the 1920s that used the headline: "And a little child shall lead them...to your product."[15] A wonderful lady called Peggy Charren, founder of Action for Children's Television, argued that all advertising addressed to children is inherently unfair and a disservice to society. The use of a beloved father figure or radio uncle or motherly creature to do the huckstering seemed to her especially reprehensible. Her warnings began to be heard.[16] Fortunately, Charren's role is being carried on by Kathryn Montgomery of the Center for Media Education, organized by Jeffrey Chester, which recently released a powerful document titled "Web of Deception." It made clear that the evils combated by Peggy Charren rise again in cyberspace, especially in numerous websites maintained by corporate America targeting the cybertot. In many families, children are more at home with computers than their parents are. Many a parent is therefore delighted to see the child logging on instead of tuning in. Isn't the computer said to be the key to a successful future? But website entertainment often blends seamlessly into merchandising and exploitation. The child is welcomed to the website as to a club. There, he or she has friends encounters wondrous creatures, can talk with television heroes and heroines, and becomes a member of something, sharing secret rituals and codes, and may be given special club money, which can be sent in for merchandise or better yet, for a ring or a badge to show you're a member. To get these, you may have to fill out a form explaining who you are, where you live, and all about your family. As a child yields such demographic data, perhaps proudly, it may be caught in a web that blends seamlessly from entertainment to commerce to invasion of privacy. The title: *Web of Deception,* from the Center for Media Education.

But perhaps the most dangerous triumph of advertising is its gradual takeover of our election procedures, the central process of democracy. Whenever I visit my native land, the Netherlands, my cousins and nephews like to ask me how we can endure such an undemocratic system. Most leading democracies forbid the sale of time for political appeals. In most, free television time is, by law, allotted to opposing parties on some statistical basis such as: the size of a party's membership, or its representation in a legislature, or votes in a previous election. There is no reason why our broadcasting systems, enriched from publicly owned channels, should not yield time for something of such "public" importance. Must we privatize even our democratic rituals? We know the result. Money plays an almost grotesque role in the procedure. When a politician announces his candidacy for a major office, we sometimes hear it said, "He'll never make it. He can't raise the money." Even elections now seem a question to be left to market forces.

I think even Adam Smith would squirm in his grave. This patron saint of businessmen—merchants, is the term he would use—published his *Wealth of Nations* the year the Declaration of Independence was signed. Maximum freedom from restraints was his recipe for prosperity. He saw national wealth evolving from the merchant's exercise of self-interest—or rather, from the impact of many competing self-interests. He also noted that merchants are so highly respected for astuteness that many people want to give them governmental power. But this, said Smith, would be perilous. The merchant's alertness to his own self-interest is likely, Smith said, to blind him to the public interest. A government of merchants, he therefore felt, would be "the worst of all governments for any people whatever."

Struggles between public and private interests have a long history in our society and are moving rapidly into a new arena. Decisions made early in such periods are likely to hang on, as we have seen. People living in the midst of such currents and whirlpools may be hard put to understand them and what they signify. Historians will study and restudy them endlessly. Fortunately, they are beginning the process.

Notes

1   Rhodes, F.L., *Beginnings of Telephony* (N.Y.: Harper, 1929) 197.

2   Barnouw, E., *A Tower in Babel* (N.Y.: Oxford, 1966) 94-6.

3   *Radio Broadcast* (N.Y.: Doubleday Page, monthly), May, 1922.

4   Quoted in Wallace, W.H., "The Development of Broadcasting in North Carolina, 1922-48" (Ph.D. Duke, 1962), unpublished.

5   Hoover's doubts were justified. This became clear when the case of *U.S. v. Zenith* (1926) ended in a government defeat. Zenith had defied a Hoover order on constitutional grounds. This defeat brought a period of spectrum chaos and precipitated action on a new radio law, the Radio Act of 1927, which created the Federal Radio Commission.

6   The text was published in Archer, G., *History of Radio: to 1926* (N.Y., American Historical Society, 1938) 397-8.

7   Barnouw, E., *The Sponsor* (N.Y.: Oxford, 1978) 19.

8   Herring, E.P., "Politics and Radio Regulation," *Harvard Business Review*, January 1935.

9   Barnouw, E., *A Tower in Babel* (N.Y.: Oxford, 1966) 174.

10 A 1952 amendment to the Communications Act *forbade* the FCC, when acting on transfer proposals, to consider "...whether the public interest, convenience and necessity might be served by the transfer, assignment, and disposal of the permit or license to a person other than the proposed transferee or licensee."

11 Soon after GE took over NBC, network staffers received a request to contribute to GE's Political Action Committee "to ensure that the company is well represented in Washington..." The letter added: "Employees who elect not to participate in a giving program of this type should question their own dedication to the company and their own expectations." See further Barnouw, E., *Tube of Plenty* (N.Y.: Oxford, 1990 ed.) 510-11.

12 *Broadcasting*, February 1, 1932.

13 De Forest's letter to the *Chicago Tribune*, October 28, 1946.

14 *Broadcasting*, April 19, 1954.

15 Quoted in Seldes, Gilbert, *The Public Arts* (N.Y.: Simon & Schuster, 1956) 252.

16 The National Association of Broadcasters (NAB) did its best to ward off the criticism over commercialized children's programs. As in other disputes, it did so via a Roper poll, which in 1971 asked 1993 people: "How do you feel—that there should be *no* commercials on any children's programs or that it is all right to have them if they don't take unfair advantage of children?" The magazine *Transaction* commented: "The saving grace of that last clause! A poll-taker's masterpiece—to insert as a given that which is in dispute." With the stated proviso, 74 percent of the 1993 people said it would be "all right to have them." The NAB headlined its report on this result: "ROPER FINDS THAT THREE OUT OF FOUR AMERICANS APPROVE PRINCIPLE OF COMMERCIAL SPONSOR-SHIP FOR CHILDREN'S TELEVISION PROGRAMS." The poll was based on home interviews.

Richard M. Cohen

THE CORPORATE TAKEOVER OF NEWS

Blunting the Sword

There was a book. Journalists once frequently consulted that book at a great news organization called CBS News. Management demanded that. They told us to read it and learn it and take it very seriously. The other networks must have had their versions of that document.

Ours was called *Standards and Practices*. *Standards and Practices* was our bible, laying out a strict code of journalism. It was a detailed guide to what was and was not acceptable, indeed permissible, in news gathering and the production of news. Quite simply, it was who we were, an identity now gathering dust and forgotten and only mentioned in the past tense.

There was a wall. That wall stood strong. The wall was impenetrable. The corporation respected it. The wall stood between the newsroom and the boardroom. It separated church and state, cathedral and cash register.

And there was a mission called television news.

We live in the continuing age of television. Viewers are bombarded by images in an electronic culture where what we see drowns out what we hear. Most of what we know about ourselves is dispensed on the tube. We live in a time when perception quickly becomes more powerful than truth. If we didn't see it on television, it didn't happen.

These days television news is the source of most perceptions in the public mind. TV chronicles history in the present tense. Television news has an important job to do and, I believe, has become an institution that fails America everyday.

Television news is glorified and romanticized. It glows bright, with that New York aura of glamour. Popular culture elevates TV news to show business, what discerning viewers might consider the down elevator. TV's anchors ride around in limousines, its stars grandly clothed in high fashion. The curious are more likely to see the brightest stars of television news on the pages of *People* than in any journalism review in a decent library.

I thought our job in news was just to tell Americans the hard truth. The facts. What you need to know about your world. That's what the press is supposed to do, is it not? To insert ourselves under the citizens' skin and infect them with that virus of everything they probably don't really want to deal with but very much need to know.

There's no cause for alarm or discomfort though. This is a new era of television. It doesn't work that way anymore. In television, journalism is no longer a calling. It's a big deal job with a fat paycheck. Objectives have changed. We are audience-driven now. We're not mission-driven: propelled by our responsibility to inform. We're just here to entertain, to soothe. We're here to sell our wares.

Gone are the torn corduroy sport jackets and holes in our shoes. Now, journalists wear the same grey suits, the same natty cravats, as the people we are covering. We're players now and probably attending the same fashionable dinner parties as the movers and shakers whom we will interview tomorrow.

There is a serious problem with television news today. It's not doing its job.

Everyone seems to hate the press. Most of us are especially critical of television news. All of us in America own TVs, and we tune in incessantly. Everyone is a TV critic. Well, go ahead and hate the press, loathe television news. But, please do it for the right reasons. Don't just drag up every old shibboleth about the conniving, conspiring liberal media. Spare us your theories about television's manipulative positions on issues, our secret leftist social agendas. I'd like to meet all these lefties in America's newsrooms.

Besides, anyone who has ever visited a newsroom and television studio learns TV's real secret. It is nothing short of a miracle that news programs manage to get on the air at the appointed hour every night, nevermind to be produced with a slant.

The fact is, television news would never bother to have a slant. TV has no agenda, except to be profitable. Toward that end, TV news is supportive of establishments, usually almost by inertia. TV cannot sell successfully to an audience that is more provoked than pleased, more challenged than cheered. That's the conventional wisdom of the news managers who sign our paychecks.

TV's only ax to grind is its demand to try to earn large profits. The problem is, the more market driven news becomes, the greater its determination not to rock the boat. The common denominator keeps dropping. Pretty soon, television news is painting by numbers.

The oft-repeated conspiracy theories about news are not the nature of the problem, indeed, they miss the point. The loud complaint about television news ought to be this: TV news doesn't serve the public interest. Corporate ownership of the networks and local stations is destroying the integrity of news.

The dumbing down, the demise of news is all about the hunger for advertising revenues and how that plays out in the newsroom. It's about the decline of news values. Altered objectives. The real crisis in television news today is about corporate control and the emerging corporate culture.

That is no less true in the newspaper and newsmagazine world, though, given the power of television, its brand of news deserves special attention. Broadcasting has lived through almost two decades of diminished seriousness and clout as news managers dabble in entertainment values and the irrelevant, instead of solid news values and what is important, to sell their product. And it is only getting worse.

In 1986, The General Electric Corporation purchased RCA, the parent corporation of the National Broadcasting Company for $6.28 billion. NBC News, of course, is only one division of NBC. This was once the network of Huntley/Brinkley. NBC News was a serious place. RCA was no stranger to the Pentagon. But GE is a huge corporate entity that feeds off the defense establishment and is better known for cost overruns than television reruns.

Actor Ronald Reagan told America forty years ago that at GE progress is our most important product. We believed him. By the eighties, the corporate move into communications was already underway. GE's was a significant move forward, if forward is the direction it took.

One year earlier, the American Broadcasting Company had been acquired by Capitol Cities Communications. Cap Cities, at least, was already in the communications business. And communications was not only their most important product, it was their only product. There was some comfort in that. Then, in 1995, the mouse roared. Disney swallowed up Cap Cities and The American Broadcasting Company and, of course, ABC News for $19 billion in one, giant gulp. Communications corporations were devouring their own. This acquisition created an enormous conglomerate, a magic media kingdom of its own.

ABC News employees soon were addressed in company memos as "cast members," from Diane Sawyer to desk assistants, Peter Jennings to production assistants. Disney got flak for that and dropped the policy. But if you walked into ABC News headquarters on West 66th last summer, there it was, larger than life and right there in the lobby for all the world to see: a large 3-D cut out of the Hunchback of Notre Dame. Diane, Peter, and the Hunchback. Just one big, happy media family. And don't forget Goofy.

In late 1995, the last shoe dropped. CBS, once known as the Tiffany network, was bought by the Westinghouse Corporation for

$5.4 billion. That's a fire sale price. CBS was now the J.C. Penney network. CBS News had been eviscerated and almost wiped out by Laurence Tisch, the previous owner, and no one knew what would happen next. The fat was long gone. So was some of the muscle. So, there it is—Westinghouse and General Electric, sisters in the nuclear family. The defense establishment. And now news. No conflict of interest there.

The circle is almost complete. Ruppert Murdoch is expanding News Corp., though his nose for news seems forever clogged, his intentions forever unclear. So far, the tabloid show *A Current Affair* is the closest Murdoch has come to news on his broadcast network. Now, he's bringing his touch to cable news. The Australian media mogul talks a good game, but Fox has never matched Murdoch's rhetoric with serious news programming.

Time/Warner has absorbed CNN. The Clinton administration threatened to block the merger for awhile, but that seemed to be lip service. Lip service is a specialty of government regulators such as the Federal Communications Commission and the Federal Trade Commission. At the end of the day, these commissioners reside in the pockets of the very industries they are supposed to regulate. The FCC staff didn't like the merger. They said it was not in the public interest. The staff didn't get to vote.

This is not the news business many idealistic young journalists went into because we wanted to make a difference. The financial stakes now are astronomical. Some would say, obscene. And broadcast news may have been changed forever.

In macroeconomics, we learn the difference between cyclical change, with its ebbs and flows, and structural change. The letter is permanent, sort of like death. The infrastructure of news has been altered. The cement is dry, the building built. No ebbs and flows here. This is low tide.

It is not enough to simply note this extraordinary concentration of media power. It has been going on in the newspaper world for a long time. Ben Bagdikian's seminal work, *The Media Monopoly,* laid that out years ago. Instead of screaming that the sky is falling in, it's time to take the next step and ask, so what? What does this corporate lock on television mean for us, for the news consumer? What does it mean for the nation?

It means a lot and matters more because news has been altered to sell and we are an under-informed public. We hear a lot about the news boom. News is everywhere, from cable to all-news radio. But the boom is quantitative, not qualitative. Sure, there is a ton of news. It's everywhere. It's all the same, though, and shallow, being prepared by the same, tired commercial cookbook in the hope that you'll buy it. How do you like *News Lite*? It's less filling.

The corporate culture has met the news culture. They are, and are supposed to be, diametrically opposed to each other. Neither can function with integrity or effectiveness when they merge. I argue that news has been redefined by the marketplace in its own image. News values, once no-frills, no-nonsense, have been recast according to corporate perceptions of what sells. That means the arrogant, elitist old news culture has been overtaken by the Stepford system of pandering to please viewers. Take it from a producer. Producers produce. Producers stoke the fires in the engine room every day. We know what goes into the furnace.

Newsroom arguments before airtime used to center on questions of what was most important to tell viewers. Now it is, what do viewers want to hear? What will they stay with? Nielsen measures viewership in ten minute increments. A viewer staying is more important to the broadcaster than one merely tuning in.

As a news producer, I want you to understand the consequences of ratings-driven news, what it means and how it plays out. In a TV universe where every rating point represents close to a million dollars in advertising revenue every day, competition is intense. With network viewership declining precipitously—and that includes the evening news—survival depends on hanging onto viewers. That desperate objective produces ratings-driven news, designed to soothe and please more than to inform and challenge.

News promises a lot. Give us twenty-two minutes, and we'll give you the world. W-I-N-S, WINS all-news radio makes that same deal with listeners every hour of every day. They've been doing it for years. Do they deliver? Of course not. That preposterous promise is news hype. The construct of self-importance is emblematic of electronic hubris, the broadcasting baloney and news come-on that is hurled at us every day.

Twenty-two minutes. That's known as the news window, now down to twenty-one minutes on television. And we'll give you the world? You'll be lucky to get a few counties of New Jersey. The news window is the nonadvertising portion of the broadcast, that unfortunate, obligatory news programming between commercials.

The fast-paced cutting in news, the quick edits came about as the pace of the ads picked up. Now, both have become impressionistic, and they are practically subliminal. This is no way to deliver or have to take in serious news.

Soundbites used to be long. When a heckler tormented Senator Edmund Muskie in his 1968 bid to be vice president, Muskie invited the student to the podium. That night, the networks ran that young man's diatribe for one full minute on the evening news. Today, he wouldn't get ten seconds. Soundbites are no longer informational. They are only punctuational. Soundbites are merely production devices. Three-second bursts from someone are not unusual. Imagine what television would do to, say, the Gettysburg Address.

And remember this?: And that's the way it is.

That nightly assertion was slightly inflated. It did come from one of the good guys, the old man of the news mountain, Walter Cronkite. But Walter told viewers every night they had gotten more than he ever could have delivered in that short time. But America had no reason not to believe him.

Networks flirted with the idea of one hour news a decade ago. Now they are fighting for their lives with their paltry twenty-one minutes. Together, they have under 60 percent of households with TVs. There used to be widespread speculation in the news business that sooner or later—maybe sooner—one network would go out of the news business and make a lot of money in the process. Now, some insiders shake their heads and wonder when a network will cease to be. The landscape is changing rapidly.

Television news is a tough business. It has been selling itself for close to fifty years. It promises and promotes to sell, sell, sell a product vital to democracy. News is the only constitutionally protected product in America. News matters, though today, it is treated as just another commodity.

The real news pitch ought to be: "Attention, K-Mart shoppers." A K-Mart shopper is someone who wants something for as close to nothing as is possible. As news consumers, most of us are, in fact, K-Mart shoppers. A news K-Mart shopper is someone who will not read a good newspaper every day and probably doesn't open a bad one. This K-Mart shopper doesn't touch a news magazine. For this shopper depends on television. TV news. This passive approach to being informed, with it's casual watching and easy listening should take care of the whole package. It's got to be easy.

Maybe we Americans get what we pay for and deserve what we get.

Well, attention K-Mart shoppers: Beware of the flawed, frail delivery system of news dispensed on the tube. If this is it, if this is your only window on your world, you should know what you are getting and why it's coming to you that way. Our treasured democracy has been placed in the way of danger by news that under-informs, sold to a population that doesn't know enough about itself to exercise its choices.

Walter Lippman, a journalist and writer, in his 1922 book, *Public Opinion,* defined news as a picture of reality on which men can act. The gender anachronism was revised by Fred Friendly up at Columbia, who rewrote Lippman—Fred would rewrite anyone—the new version calling news a portrait of reality on which the citizen can act.

The point is, Lippman defined news as relevant information. News has utilitarian value. In a free society, news is fuel. News is blood. We are a society of choices. We are citizens with a franchise. We need to know our world, which means understanding our nation and our own backyards. That is as important as sorting out Bosnia, Beirut, and Beijing.

With that reality as a backdrop, answer this. What is the purpose of news in America today? To enlighten and edify? Perhaps. No. The purpose of news is to make money, to generate corporate profits. Pretty high-minded, isn't it? We're not talking about mom-and-pop operations here. Especially with television, we are talking about corporate America and profit expectations as high as 40 percent. Small businesses survive with single digit profit margins. For a modest business, a 15 percent profit means it was a banner year.

What is happening in communications is the same story of run-amuck corporate cannibalism terrorizing most of American business. The Darwinian process of mergers and acquisitions began to wash over the corporate landscape in the 1980s. We all observed small companies eaten by bigger companies and devoured by even more mammoth corporate interests. This has become the new food chain of capitalism.

But, if we are to accept the Lippman definition of news, if we agree on the critical importance of news in American society, then this concentration of power in the news business takes on special importance with devastating consequences. I argue that the content of news has changed from what is important to what sells, which means it is no longer pure news at all. The utilitarian value of news has been decimated.

How we got to this point on the map, the evolution of television news, is a complex story. It is a romantic journey that began in the Second World War and catapulted TV news toward the end of the century. Students of broadcast journalism can skip Murrow, and Collingwood, and Cronkite and, instead, focus on some different names. Tisch. Turner. Even Reagan. These giants—actually, *Spy* magazine always referred to Tisch as the billionaire dwarf—these men were not necessarily heroes, but they walked paths that would intersect and change broadcasting.

It was 1980. Along came cable and Ted Turner. Turner unveiled CNN. There was giggling in newsrooms all over New York. We sneered, snickered, and scoffed. Then, Ted Turner ate our lunch. CNN was on the map and opening bureaus around the world, even as networks were beginning to close theirs. News was Turner's only product.

William S. Paley, the founder of CBS, Inc., had traveled from a family that made cigars to a home known as Black Rock. Paley unequivocally backed his news division. He knew CBS News would be the public face of the corporation, the loss leader, which got people into the store. Paley loved his news division and didn't care if it made money.

Today, wishful thinkers speculate that Westinghouse and GE, Disney and News Corp., will seek that same credibility only news offers. That credibility is expensive, and history suggests these corporations will seek only revenues. The marketplace is crowded now. This is a different era. Who needs respectability, or who can afford it?

When Paley's power faded in the 1980s, and the old lions who were his competitors died off, rules and expectations changed. Journalists learned a new term, "profit center," as the bean counters, the guys with the calculators, started pushing for lower costs and higher profits. Now, they held the power.

There is the wonderful story about the time high-priced consultants from Coopers and Lybrand, management experts all, converged on the CBS News Bureau in London. Their mission was to make recommendations on how to streamline the operation; you know, cut costs. They asked a tape editor what he was doing.

"Cutting a story for the evening news," came the straightforward reply.

"But you did that yesterday," came the incredulous follow up. This particular bean counter didn't even know that the news shark has to be fed every day, sometimes twice a day. And these people are in charge of your viewing habits.

News is a business. News always has been a business in this country. Selling newspapers is as old an enterprise as printing them. News has to make a profit. Most journalists have no problem with that. No one wants government anywhere near a printing press or television camera. But this exploding pressure for profits was new, and the not-so-slow invention of ratings-driven news followed.

At the Big Three networks, a new breed of bottom-line dwellers had taken control. At CBS News, in 1981, this took the form of a charismatic, corpulent corporate player named Van Gordon Sauter. Van resembled Santa Claus, even as he was making his Faustian bargain with the powers-that-be.

Santa had presents for us all. He made a circus of the morning news and softened the evening news, telling us he wanted news that "makes people feel good about themselves." Excuse me? I believe that's the mission of the social engineer. It's a far cry from honest journalism.

In fairness, Van was the first CBS News president to live with the post-Paley ratings pressure. Toward that end, Van really did make a mockery of the venerable *CBS Morning News,* and he pressured us to watch a program that he considered the wave of the future. It was called *Entertainment Tonight.* We, of course, told him we thought it was the most important new program on television. We understood that emerging reward system. We wanted to get ahead, and we knew our turns would come.

The reward system in any business goes a long way toward defining the product. It was no different at CBS News. We may not have liked what we saw, what was going on around us. There can be compelling personal reasons, such as financial obligations, which weigh in against rocking the boat. Nothing blunts a journalist's sword like a mortgage.

What's important here is that networks watch and imitate each other all the time. CBS was diminishing its content, bastardizing its news in pursuit of ratings. The others were not far behind. A word that comes to mind is pandering, changing identities for specific purposes.

Lesley Stahl was CBS's White House correspondent throughout most of the seventies and eighties. Lesley now admits that Sauter forced her to soften up on Ronald Reagan. Reagan was popular, she was told, and viewers are going to turn us off if we criticized him too much.

Calvin Coolidge had warned us. The business of America is business. News is all business now and not about to let some old values a few of us hold dear stand in the way. The 1980s became the era that saw news redefined.

So, along came Laurence Tisch, Chairman of the Loew's Corporation and possible white knight for news. But that was not to be. Tisch didn't care about news. His passion was reserved for the balance sheets. Tisch demonstrated a special fondness for black ink, a commitment to bring costs into line. His line. So CBS closed news bureaus all over the world. Paris and Rome. Closed. Warsaw and Johannesburg. Gone. Hong Kong and Bangkok, Bonn and Beirut. Finished. And the list goes on.

Just go across Manhattan. Networks used to maintain bureaus at the United Nations. How expensive could that have been? Richard C. Hotellet was CBS's U.N. correspondent at that time. Hotellet had covered the war in Europe for CBS Radio and was in Paris when the Allies liberated the city. Richard took his U.N. assignment as seriously, more seriously, than CBS did. When was the last time anyone saw a U.N. report on the evening news, except when the president of the United States was there?

In 1987, Laurence Tisch fired hundreds of employees. A lot of good journalists got their walking papers. Over two hundred were executed in one bloodletting alone. The other networks made similar moves, though with fewer casualties and less attention.

News was now to be packaged in London or Tokyo, with footage fed in and edited in those cities, far from many of the stories. Reporters who were not even at the scene now write the scripts. Eyes and ears on the ground, Murrow on the rooftops of London during the blitzkrieg was the great reportorial tradition at CBS. No more. The networks reported Bosnia from London for a long time, when they reported it at all.

Martha Teichner reported Bosnia from London, it seemed, forever. I know Martha. She would have been on a plane to the region in a flash if CBS had been willing to pay for the ticket. Eventually, when the body count got high enough in Bosnia, the networks did go in for firsthand reporting.

When ABC News doesn't bother reporting a story from the story, it's obvious. A viewer just has to listen to the sign off. It will say, "So-and-so, ABC News." Period. There is no dateline offered, no city. That invariably means the reporter is in New York. It's not always obvious. News consumers have to watch carefully and think, if it matters to them at all.

At CBS, some of us in the newsroom began to joke that we had studied at the Columbia Graduate School of Packaging. That is what we were doing. Packaging. Too often we sarcastically said, "it'll be okay. It looks like news." We really were told by executives to make it look like news. Half-facetious. Yes, and half true. Too true.

TV news was going downhill rapidly. But, the point isn't poor us. It's poor you. You are citizens and news consumers, and you need that nightly portrait of reality. You are in charge of your lives and have to act in national elections in alternating Novembers, more frequently at the local level.

Here's your problem: television news doesn't like Washington. Doesn't like stories about government. They are presumed boring. Van Sauter hated Washington. He demagogued and railed against it the way his idol, Ronald Reagan, did. In the old days, there probably had been too great a reliance on the nation's capital, too many stories about Congressional hearings. Now we couldn't get anything from D.C. on the air.

And TV really doesn't like presidential or any other form of politics. Management wisdom says they are all a turnoff. Literally. Choosing the president of the United States is arguably the most important story in the world. It matters. Can you imagine news executives pressuring the evening news to go easy on presidential politics? I saw it happen at CBS News. My friends at other networks went through the same thing.

My demise at CBS News came after Dan Rather's celebrated interview with then Vice President George Bush on the facts about the

Iran-Contra escapade. What had Bush known? The interview disintegrated into a shouting match between Rather and the vice president,
who claimed we had misled him about the subject of the interview.

We hadn't. I set up and choreographed the video battle. Whatever
one thought about Bush or what we did, CBS, Inc., was furious with
us. Station managers were complaining loudly to the network. They
said we had made viewers angry at CBS, and they feared TV watch-
ers would tune CBS out. That would be death by the dial.

The corporation didn't care about the journalism involved. They
only cared that station managers and, ostensibly, viewers were not
happy. Vice President Bush had been lying when he claimed to be
"out of the loop" on Iran-Contra. But the televised confrontation was
simply bad for business. CBS News was kind enough to allow me to
leave by the door.

When TV does grudgingly tackle politics and elections, television
news usually takes the path of pleasing viewers, or displeasing them
least. TV portrays campaigns as horse races, reducing important elections to sporting events. So, it's who's up, who's down. And let's do
our own poll, manufacture our own news.

The civic problem with polls as news, of course, is that these public opinion samplings are but a snapshot of the moment, and are
likely to change mercurially. Perceptions about specific candidates as
winners or losers, however, are set in cement in the public mind too
early in the process.

News organizations' polls are frequently self-promotional
and have little use as news, especially months, even weeks, before
the voting, and they can provide self-fulfilling prophecies. Whose
interest does that serve? The real issues are invariably important
but stay on some tiny back burner. News executives think issues
are boring.

So, if you are wondering why presidential elections are shallow
and seem hardly worth following, you should decide who is at fault.
Point your finger at the politicians, then step back and point it directly
at the television cameras.

Campaigns are run for those cameras. From candidate schedules to soundbites, the whole operation revolves around TV. TV's deadlines and its hunger for pictures are what campaigns are all about. It's too easy to simply blame the candidates for the low common denominator of politics.

It's not just politics that suffers from inadequate coverage. TV doesn't deal with international stories very well. Television news does not have a strong commitment to foreign news. It's a turnoff. Who should pop up with that message last autumn but Andy Rooney. Rooney said on *60 Minutes* that network news is not doing its job. Rooney cited the shortage of foreign news as evidence.

So, here we are in this electronic era, with diminished personnel and news gathering capabilities and definite ideas about diluting content. Producers are forced to second-guess what kind of news, what sorts of stories will hold an audience. Our jobs depend on it. We are caught between standing for something and surviving.

Rock, meet hard place.

This is all about ownership. It's about profit expectations—the demand to make a buck. For a network or local journalist to stand up and say "no," is for that person to take the consequences. I fought what I considered the good fight, and I was flicked off the corporate shoulder like a fly.

Pretend you are the executive producer of an evening news broadcast. You know that you are tired of business as usual, all the pandering and compromising. You are going to do it right. Of course, your bosses watch all three evening news broadcasts simultaneously. They see something sexy on another network, something you refused to run on some principle, the executive hotline buzzes and you get an earful. The second time, you get a pink slip.

Does that sound paranoid? It's not paranoia if they really are out to get you. Actually, they are not out to get us, only out to get what they want, cooked precisely to their tastes. There's only one cookbook in television news, and it belongs to them.

What news managers really crave is the perfect story, the ideal news item. Newsroom nonsense always defined the perfect story as anything dealing with pets, tits, or tots. There are variations. When our metaphorical news truck pulls into the station for fuel, it pulls up to one of two pumps. One reads, great pictures; the other, high emotion. The news truck takes on all the fuel it can hold.

The lead piece on the evening news is invariably picture-driven. The picture bias skews editorial decisions when footage is strong on one story with scant footage on another, even if that one is a more important story than the first. Sometimes, great pictures create a story even when there is no real news. Really good pictures in the lead story will capture and keep viewers. That's the wisdom. I've never believed it. I think folks just want the news.

Sometimes, we get picture stories just for their own sake. Dan Rather, in an anchor voice-over, once described a dramatic refinery fire in New Jersey. It was a spectacular fire, on the Hudson across from New York. We showed strong footage of exploding flames against the black of night. There were silhouettes of firemen working feverishly to fight the blaze. And Rather concluded by casually saying that there were no deaths, no injuries. He should have added, no news, either. This is not peculiar to CBS or to Dan Rather. Networks all report the same kinds of stories.

At the same time, television backs off stories that are visually weak. If there are no pictures, there probably will be no prominent place on the evening news. That's why television news does so badly on economic news or anything else that is subtle. In television, subtle we're not.

Television likes good guys and bad guys, black hats and white hats. The trouble with that, of course, is that the world is grey. Television news is reductionist. We simplify, then simplify our simplification. *60 Minutes* has been dining out on that for years.

The selection of stories to highlight, the news networks lead with and thrust into national prominence, has gradually changed in more than a decade of escalating competitive pressures and the explicit demand for ratings success. Consider two case studies: the stories of two Jessicas, nine years apart.

Jessica Dubroff, a beautiful little girl who perished in a small plane. She was making her way across the country last April in search of a record. And Jessica McClure, an eighteen-month-old child at the time. This Jessica disappeared down a twenty-two foot, abandoned water well near the oil fields of Midland, Texas. You may remember her story.

The Jessica McClure ordeal took precisely two days to play out in October, 1987. That was right smack in the middle of the era of changing news values. Jessica McClure offers an extraordinary laboratory for examining the values that drive commercial TV news and the clear bias of selection.

Jessica disappeared, and it was established quickly enough that she had gone down that tiny, tomb-like pipe deep into the dry earth. Americans were instantly mesmerized by the drama of the rescue effort. A second hole had to be dug down deep and a connection made for the rescue. Networks went on the air, and they stayed on. At one point, Dan Rather held up a stovepipe to show how narrow that well was. Jessica McClure's rescue turned into one of the highest-rated events in television history.

CNN, alone, captured over three million households at one point in the crisis. CNN holds about five hundred thousand viewers at any given moment on a good day. Fifty-eight hours into the siege, Jessica was brought to the surface by paramedic Robert O'Donnell. O'Donnell did the job, despite a serious case of claustrophobia, because he was slender and the only qualified person who would fit down that hole. Jessica McClure was alive. People all over America celebrated.

This was an extraordinary event. But let's get tough here. Put on your green eyeshades and play news editor. Was this an appropriate lead for a national newscast? It took up a third to half of available news time for a few days.

The news window—remember, that's the editorial, nonadvertising time—was under twenty-two minutes even then. Are you going to give six or seven or more of those precious minutes to a human interest story revolving around one life?

Consider what else was happening in the third week in October 1987. When Jessica fell down that hole, the stock market had just crashed. The country's financial infrastructure was in doubt. Missiles were being fired at U.S. tankers in the Persian Gulf. Mikhail Gorbachev was proposing *glasnost* to the United States. Oliver North was testifying in the first Iran-Contra trial, and Senator Gary Hart's celebrated relationship with Donna Rice was being unveiled. And let's not forget Tammy Faye and Jim Bakker, whose illegal activities were unfolding.

A lot was going on. Most of it was news we could use, news that would have to be called important. It's not that little Jessica McClure should have been ignored. Television news should have offered a little perspective, though. But the news truck was in the station. It was stopped at the high emotion pump, and it took on a lot of fuel that week.

The problem for the evening news and its viewers is that for every story that is broadcast, two or three are left out. Much more news is gathered in a single day than can ever fit on the evening news. When you have a news window that is now twenty-one minutes, and you devote seven or eight minutes to a single story, you are going to leave a lot of other news unreported.

One postscript: Robert O'Donnell, the skinny, brave paramedic who went down and got Jessica McClure to safety suffered from severe depression after the event. O'Donnell said he never would have gone down there if he had known what kind of media scrutiny would follow. O'Donnell took his own life eight years later, very much the victim of media overkill.

And, Nancy Reagan was in the hospital, having been diagnosed with breast cancer. Mrs. Reagan is said to have refused to leave her TV for treatment until Jessica was brought up.

For those who ask "What's wrong with this picture? Viewers are just getting what they want," the very definition of news is called into question. News is supposed to tell people what they need to know, not just show them what they want to see. A real journalist shouldn't care what they want to see. They can spend their money and go to the movies for that.

This illustrates a basic conflict with market-driven news. It questions what values should define news. Should they be the entertainment values that say give people what they want, or the news values that say give viewers what they need? That used to be an easy one. The high road was our highway, but in the world of ratings-driven news, there are conflicts and contradictions everywhere. Just staying on the road is a battle.

If network news is flirting heavily with disrepute, local news executives are proudly wearing the scarlet "A" on their chests, "A" for acquiescence to entertainment pressures. There is simply nothing local news won't do for ratings, especially in larger markets. No city in America offers consumers worse news about news than New York. The network-owned stations there even manufacture news stories to play off of network movie offerings.

When CBS broadcast *In Cold Blood* last November, based on Truman Capote's account of a sensational family murder in Kansas, WCBS did splashy stories about the crime. The murders were very old news, the news stories no news at all. It was, however, a fine example of cross-pollination of Hollywood and news. It's called synergy at Disney.

Then, there is the well-established role of market research in news. In television, that data is used to tell producers what kinds of stories interest viewers. Then reporters are ordered to go out and do them in the hopes that more people will watch. That is not how intelligent viewers should want a newscast to be put together.

Market research is why network news can look so local, even gimmicky. ABC's *World News Tonight* presents the *"Person of the Week"* in its third section on Friday nights. If the tribute appears to be civic-minded and inspirational, it is, in fact, only a ratings device. Consultants pointed out to ABC News management that there is a ratings drop off just before seven on Friday nights as viewers get their weekends going. The mysterious *"Person of the Week"* is simply intended to hold an audience for a few more minutes.

For a while, CBS's economic correspondent was their "money correspondent." That made the news appear less elitist.

It's true that nobody elects reporters and news editors and executive producers. These days, they just pander their way to the top of the corporate news ladder. Machines don't choose the news to report. Human beings make those decisions. People frequently complain that news is elitist. News is elitist because it has to be. News people can't hold a plebescite everyday to determine the lead on the evening news and headline in the morning paper. The tradition always was to give citizens the tough medicine. That's why we're all considered so mean and heartless. Not anymore. We're nice guys, just here to entertain you.

Michael Deaver, Ronald Reagan's media wizard, told Bill Moyers in an interview, "you people say you're in the news business. You're in the entertainment business."

The sad story of seven-year-old Jessica Dubroff was entertaining in a horrible way. In the days prior to her flight, television paraded Jessica out and simply celebrated the new, tiny Amelia Earhardt. It was pure pageantry. When her plane went down, TV immersed itself in grief. The camera was like a politician at a funeral. It was everywhere. This Jessica, too, took over the airwaves, commanded the cables. Who had wondered about safety before the accident? Who had been asking why a seven-year-old was being allowed to fly a plane, especially through the obvious bad weather?

Jessica didn't win her record. Television won its prize.

The playing field slopes at a new angle. What do people want to see? What will they stick with? What is the "Hey, Martha" story we used to search for at CBS? That was the story that was so riveting that viewers would yell to Martha across the back fence to ask if she had seen it.

No story in recent memory contained the victim quotient of TWA Flight #800. In the initial days after the crash, there were haunting questions about what had happened. First, of course, what had brought the plane down? What had witnesses seen? What parts of the plane divers might expect to find and what the days and weeks in the salt water would do to the wreckage were unknown.

One could be as fearful of Carl Ichon and his successors as of Muammar Quaddafi. TWA had been in severe financial trouble long before Ichon bailed out. The airline had a terrible maintenance record. I kept waiting for someone to piece all of that together.

What we got, especially from television, was the parade of victims. Sixteen members of the French Club with five chaperones from Montoursville High in Pennsylvania. A Harvard hockey star who had just proposed by phone to his girlfriend in Paris. An ABC sports producer who perished with his wife and one of their three kids.

It was heartbreaking, but the victim watch was the easy part. Let's get out there and scratch the surface. This coverage was television going for the heart. What about the head? There was so much we needed to learn, and TV wasn't helping us do that.

What is especially troubling is when commercial considerations cloud coverage on big stories and television news unthinkingly alters the outcome of a story. There can be policy consequences to coverage. Recent wars have been waged by the United States with television in mind. Grenada was a good example, with television's impact and American patience in mind. Sometimes the policy fallout from press pandering changes history.

Not enough has been written about coverage of the Persian Gulf War, especially because it never seems to end. President George Bush told Americans in August of 1990 that he was sending U.S. troops to Saudi Arabia to make sure Iraq didn't go beyond Kuwait, which Iraq had already invaded. No one said a word. Neither the press nor the politician.

The press used to frequently lead the political community in raising questions and doubts. We wanted to bask in the glow of patriotism, and we quickly got on board. We had alienated the citizenry with tough reports from Vietnam through Grenada, and then

Panama. Now we were not going to make that mistake again. It's bad for business.

Broadcast news cheered our boys on. We ignored suggestions by military analysts that Iraqi soldiers had actually turned their backs to the Saudi border and were digging in defensively. No. This would be like WW2. We got behind it. WCBS all-news radio organized a letter-writing campaign to keep morale high over there. NBC News began showing grinning U.S. soldiers at their stations, waving to the cameras. They'd yell out their names and where they were from. Sometimes they threw in a positive, patriotic comment. These became NBC's news bumpers. Bumpers are the pictures or graphics leading into commercials.

This is not journalism. It's jingoism, market-driven and thoughtless. It's just that pleasing viewers comes first; profits come before citizen responsibility. Don't tell me ownership, with its pressure for those profits, is not the cutting issue with news.

Dissent leading up to the Gulf War was absent and overdue. Democrats on Capitol Hill, already a timid lot, remained silent. By the time the loyal opposition turned off their TVs and wandered outdoors, wondering aloud what the hell we were doing, bombs were falling on Baghdad.

Many argue that little was accomplished in that war. The Clinton administration is fighting the same beast that Bush fought before. We propped up Kuwait, a feudal fiefdom, but Sadam remained in power and continues to work his magic, especially on the Kurds.

I argue the press is partly to blame for the whole mess. Where were we when the tough questions needed to be asked? Busy demonizing the demon Sadam. We, the press, were players. Period.

I was at CNN at the time. Some called this short war CNN's war. Bernie was in Baghdad and we were buckling under, putting government handouts on the air everyday. The war was being reported from the White House and the Pentagon and an information center in Saudi. I heard no attribution. We reported everything as if we had seen it with our own eyes. We actually saw none of it.

My friend, CBS's Bob Simon, grew so uncomfortable with the tight controls on the press that he tried to slip away and was held by the Iraqis through the entire war. Our portrait of reality had been painted over. Pentimento.

Years earlier, CBS News had led the charge, over-committing to coverage of the civil war in El Salvador and the larger war on the Contras in Nicaragua. Ronald Reagan had assumed the presidency only weeks before Dan Rather assumed the anchor chair. Both needed that war for separate reasons. War makes good television, and Rather, like Reagan, was not about to fail. Ratings war is hell.

This has everything to do with ownership, but the forces are subtle and difficult to see. It's not that some corporate executive says, "don't be critical, be patriotic." It's that reward system at work.

Everybody in the newsroom lives with the pressure for ratings. It's a way of life, like living with a disease. The company wants you to find viewers, to grow, to make more money. You take a fat pay check from the big guys every week. You have little kids and a big mortgage. You want that next promotion. Pleasing viewers makes more friends than challenging them. You don't grow by asking the rude, impertinent questions, by challenging the establishment. Just soothe them. Get them to like the anchorman. That's it. Maybe they'll watch you.

Isn't swimming upstream, asking hard questions and making folks uncomfortable what journalism is supposed to be all about? Woodward and Bernstein offended about half the political establishment in Washington. They also informed America about the most egregious political scandal in its history.

The fact is, worldwide news gathering and the dissemination of information are changing. News is being half-done today, with reluctance and at a huge cost. The future of news is the only programming that seems to keep news divisions afloat. I'm talking about prime-time news magazines.

60 Minutes, the original news magazine, was born at CBS some twenty-eight years ago. It still can get serious. Then, there are the bastard children, the pretenders. There's *20/20* and *Prime Time* on

ABC. And *Dateline*, the news magazine that's devouring NBC. *Dateline* was on the air four nights a week. NBC cut it back to three nights. Thank you, though it could be four again soon enough.

And who can forget Diane Sawyer's hard-hitting interview with "cultural terrorist" Michael Jackson? Michael Jackson is actually an entertainer. Many were offended that Sawyer and ABC News put their resources and reputations on the line with that interview. Even worse was the fact that ABC News allowed Jackson to dictate the terms of the interview, which included puff pieces on Jackson on the previous week's *Prime Time*.

If this is news, it's news to me.

Magazine shows have little to do with reality and almost nothing to do with any important national agenda. This country of ours is in a constant state of crisis over taxes and the deficit. There are deep divisions over the role of the federal government, and the budget. There are social policy disagreements that don't get resolved. Public education is going down the tubes. Children are hungry and too frequently alone. Welfare has been all but eliminated with no certain outcome. Deprivation continues as the rich get richer. And *Dateline* follows a family's cross-country trip in a van to see how vacation is going.

ABC's *20/20* offers up, "Mommy, I'm a Lesbian" for your voyeuristic, viewing pleasure.

We are fiddling while Rome burns. Dancing to Michael Jackson. We are amusing ourselves to death with news magazines which broadcast precious little of relevance. *Amusing Ourselves to Death* is the title of Neil Postman's insightful book about TV.

Television's magazines generate tremendous revenues. Apparently, a lot of people watch. Who can argue with success?

I've burned through this business. I can't do it anymore. I'm tired of looking for jobs I don't want, going to people who don't want to hire me. Who can blame them for that? I'm a bomb thrower. At least, that's what I hear. It's odd, because I merely stand for traditional values and objectives in news. I reject the new, glitzy forms of news. So, who is throwing what bombs at whom?

That's *my* problem, of course. *Yours* is a much more significant dilemma, a shared problem. You and I need to know what is going on. And no one is telling it to us straight.

What we are seeing in all network news programming is that reality just isn't good enough. Maybe this era so defined by entertainment, maybe Hollywood and the TV movie have altered our expectations, our appetites, our attention spans. Television news fills the void, by responding to public impatience, if not cynicism, by enhancing reality. Enhancing reality. It may be assumed to be the only way to keep the public in the tent.

When two jetliners collided in the sky high over India last November, ABC's *World News Tonight* began its report with what appeared to be dramatic footage. It showed an explosion and two objects in the sky—airplanes, perhaps—falling away from each other. Obviously, there were no cameras at the midair collision, so ABC was only showing viewers what the collision might have looked like, and creating the impression that they were there in the process.

At the networks in the 1980s, news was softening. At CBS News, producers came under pressure to cut entertainment footage into news stories. The theory was that movies and entertainment footage would make dry news stories sexy.

In a piece about the ongoing and endless right to die issue, we were pressured to use soap opera footage to provide drama. The sequence showed a bad actor playing a terminally ill patient in a hospice. Of course, there are many thousands of real patients in real hospices dying real deaths from real diseases all over the country. To hell with real life. We had to capture the theater of the experience.

CBS management made some deal to use as much footage from the movie *Gandhi* as we wished. So, whenever we did a story about the subcontinent, which was never, whenever we analyzed nonviolent political movements, also never, whenever we did stories about old men who wore glasses, we were pressured to take *Gandhi* footage and cut it into our piece. We practically became the *CBS Evening News with Dan Rather and Ben Kingsley.* If we balked, and some of us did, we had a private meeting with an executive who would basically tell us to get on the team.

"Oh, come on, Richard. Get off your high horse."

This is news?

The external tanks on a General Motors truck may have been dangerous enough, but that wasn't exciting enough for NBC News and *Dateline*. So they simulated a crash and blew up a vehicle themselves. It was great TV. Meanwhile, the evening news crams the proverbial ten pounds into a five-pound bag every night. It's not that news executives want you to know more. They just want it to move. The pace is surreal, the content barely comprehensible. Soundbites come in half-sentences. Ba-da-boom. It does move. If the evening news were the old Dick Clark show, the news would get a ten because the dancing never stops.

We've all been dancing as fast as we can for a long time, and I, for one, am tired. I'm done watching, at least on a regular basis. You might not be amazed to learn how many people out there are just turning off the tube. It's hard to find one broadcast that is significantly better than the others. They all dare to be the same. It's just not worth watching anymore. Who's going to turn on the television during dinner, with screaming kids and barking dogs, unless it's truly important. *Importance* is in the eye of the beholder. It is increasingly important for news consumers to understand the marketplace and know the options.

A daily paper—not every daily—and a little National Public Radio can provide a welcome shot of real news. The trouble with NPR in the morning is that we just want the facts, and they insist on taking us to a crafts fair in Oregon.

The question becomes: What, if anything, can be done? I have my doubts that anything will be done to improve television news, but something could be done. Consider two words, which represent two different approaches: *Reregulation*—recasting the Reagan tide as low tide; and AntiTrust—convincing the Justice Department and Federal Communications Commission to represent people, not industries. That, probably, can be said of most of government. Remember that quaint notion, to serve the public interest?

Broadcasting was deregulated by President Reagan on the assumption that responsible corporate behavior is good for business. Right. For decades, government had told broadcasting, you are the "guardians of the public airwaves." You have a public obligation. The Fairness Doctrine, though somewhat flawed, required broadcast licensees to deal with "controversial issues of public importance."

License renewal procedures were taken seriously by the FCC. News prospered and Americans may have had half an idea what was going on. Then President Reagan said, just kidding, to broadcasting. These are your airwaves. Go where the marketplace takes you.

The federal government could reregulate TV and put a gun to the bastards' heads. Broadcast executives need to relearn the concept of public responsibility. It has been misplaced.

There is the antitrust action that is long overdue, not to mention monopoly and anticompetitive practices prohibitions which are not enforced and have not been enforced for decades. Too few interests own too many VHF licenses. Twenty-five years ago, no single company, and that means no network, could own more than five stations. Now, there is no limit, and according to the August 19, 1996, *New York Times*, TV stations are hotter properties than ever. According to the *Times,* those acquiring the most stations now are corporations with the largest stake in television already.

One objective that is written into communications law is "a robust marketplace." That is what the Fairness Doctrine was intended to create. Another way of saying that, as the June 3, 1996 issue of *The Nation,* devoted to media monopolies points out, is the ideal of pluralism. If pluralism is to be an objective in broadcasting, there can't be five companies owning most of the airwaves.

All this country needs is an FCC willing to crawl out of the pocket of industry. The United States has enjoyed the services of precisely one public-spirited, independent FCC commissioner. He was Nicholas Johnson, appointed by President Lyndon Johnson. Nick Johnson was last spotted by this reporter at a 1988 political rally in Iowa. He was wearing a JESSE JACKSON FOR PRESIDENT T-shirt.

Mavericks don't get to regulate. They're too dangerous.

So, where does this all leave us? High and dry, unfortunately.

What about cable?

CNN has gotten its highest marks simply for existing. They are masters of the live event. CNN brings history live into living-rooms. Even their live analysis can be good, though news gathering and news programs leave something to be desired. CNN has owned cable news for over fifteen years. They've made money. Of course, they are paid twice. Once by subscribers and again by advertisers.

The fact is, CNN's growth is all overseas; their domestic audience is flat. The Time Warner acquisition of CNN has brought the specter of budget cuts, which would further dampen their ability to gather and report news.

Now, MS-NBC, Fox, and CBS are competing for those half-million households. That audience grows only in times of crisis, then shrinks again. The pie is relatively small, which makes cable news a cost game. Cable news operations must hold down costs to be at all profitable. That speaks volumes about the quality of what the new cable operations will probably be putting on the air.

The landscape is bleak. The sword has been blunted, the mission abandoned. The marketplace has triumphed, and we are all the losers. American news consumers, just another way of saying citizens, are qualitatively under informed. Available political solutions to this problem would involve crossing swords with some of the wealthiest, most powerful corporate forces in America. President Clinton and Republican leaders receive huge campaign contributions from the PACs of corporate America. There is no political incentive for them to rock the boat by challenging the status quo.

In cynical moments, one could believe the political establishment has a stake in keeping the citizenry uninformed. That allows the political class freedom and keeps the citizenry down on the farm.

So, what are we going to do? Ralph Nader taught all of us the power of consumer movements when he and his disciples forced corporate responsibility on the giant U.S. auto industry. Everyone in America is a news consumer and, remember, everyone's a critic. We can insist on better and vote with the dial on our TVs.

There ought to be a well-organized, nonpartisan, indeed, apolitical movement to force quality back into news. I doubt that's going to happen. Americans seem to have little enough consciousness of corporate control of their entire lives and no concerns about news.

We live in the shadow of that corporate monolith extending ever upward into the sky. Corporations have been called private governments, and they are becoming the state. The financial power of companies explodes around us. The small issue of news quality is probably not even on the corporate radar screen. Conglomerates only grow greedier and fatter for their own purposes.

KNOW THIS: Growth for its own sake is the ideology of the cancer cell.

Gene Roberts

CONGLOMERATES AND NEWSPAPERS

It is difficult to survey the American newspaper landscape these days and not become truly alarmed. Many, perhaps most, have squeezed and re-squeezed their newsroom budgets to the point that they no longer cover their communities well. This is a serious failure because historically newspapers have been part of the glue that holds America's counties, towns and cities and states together by keeping the citizenry informed.

Even some of the media analysts on Wall Street are becoming distress alarmed, *and* no wonder. What is happening is not only bad for the cities and communities newspapers serve, it is bad for business and ultimately for stockholders. It is hard to be more eloquent than one analyst, John Morton, was in the spring 1996 issue of *Neiman Reports*. "One would think that the newspaper business is trying to pull itself back from some final, life-threatening brink," he said. But no—all the industry is trying to do is increase its profitability from maybe two times the average of the Fortune 500 to three or four times.

"The newspaper business is truly besieged," he added. "But not from lack of profits. Circulation is waning, readership is weakening, especially among young people, and advertisers increasingly are seeking other ways to reach customers besides advertising in newspapers. The dumbest thing—the least rational thing—that any business can do when faced with so many negative trends is to cut back on quality of product and level of service. Yet this is precisely what many newspapers are doing."

There is, of course, a simple prescription for insuring the future of a newspaper—become, and remain, indispensable to the serious reader, to the person who wants to be an informed citizen, who wants real information. This means more news coverage in depth and in breadth. And this means spending more, not less, on both staff and news. Alas, many newspapers—I would argue the overwhelming majority of them—are going the other way.

There may be an eventual solution to rising newsprint and delivery costs—perhaps replicating machinery in each reader's home. But newspapers that do not keep their news gathering operations intact in the worst of times, and expanding in the best of times, will not be positioned well, if at all, for taking advantage of technological breakthroughs. In the end, a newspaper's only truly durable asset is its ability to gather information intensively and write it compellingly and understandably. There may be substitutes on the horizon for presses, so there is no insurance in presses. But a fine news gathering operation cannot be easily duplicated by any competitor. A staff big enough and talented enough to thoroughly cover its community is a reliable, trustworthy bridge to whatever the future holds.

Nothing is so reckless on the part of newspapers as what has become common practice—to shrink staff and news at every major downward move in the economy and each major upward move in newsprint prices. Economies go up as well as down, and newsprint prices go down as well as up; but readers expectations tend to remain constant. Newspapers are very much cyclical businesses. And their profits recover rapidly in good times. But the confidence of readers does not recover easily once it has been shaken by cutbacks in news coverage. And irreplaceable editors and reporters can be spooked away permanently by what they perceive to be a weakening commitment to quality. You have only to look at papers that have made deep and widely publicized cutbacks like the *Miami Herald*, the *Los Angeles Times*, and the *Philadelphia Inquirer* to understand the long-term costs of trimming staff and news to meet short-term problems such as newsprint prices, which went up and are now coming down. But many valuable staff members were so scared by the shortsightedness that they left and are not returning. These papers remain good papers, but they lost ground in news gathering that will cost more to correct in the long term, than was saved in the short run. And every time you tighten the screws on the news, you loosen the hold on serious readers. Eliminate twelve or fourteen companies in your stock listings to save one inch of newsprint and you permanently disillusion some of your regular readers. They own those stocks and each morning they are reminded that you are less complete and less reliable.

Thirty-five years ago I worked for a state capital newspaper, the *News and Observer* in Raleigh, North Carolina, that was dedicated to covering state government. When the state legislature was in session we reported on every statewide bill that was introduced and every local bill that applied to any of the approximately fifty counties in which the paper circulated. It was, let me make clear, a lot of work. It was not unusual in a single day to write three or four longish statewide stories, and then report on eight to ten local bills, giving them at least one paragraph each, and sometimes as many as five or six paragraphs. And these stories were well read. An example comes vividly to mind. One legislator introduced several bills incorporating new towns in his home county. And I wrote a little story about each bill. It would be nice to be able to say, in retrospect, that I knew something was amiss, but I did not. To the extent I thought about the bills, I imagined the legislator was turning small crossroads communities into small municipalities. But the readers in the county read my stories and figured things out. North Carolina had a law that channeled a portion of the state's gasoline taxes into municipalities for street maintenance and construction. The legislator discovered how to profit from the law. He was incorporating plowed fields and woodlands, planning to let the taxes build up until he could put in free streets for future housing developments. But because the newspaper was diligent and thorough, the voters rose up and voted the legislator out. It was democracy in action—a newspaper and voters both living up to their obligations in a democratic society.

Today, few—if any—papers would devote that much staff time and news to state coverage. But this may be a reason why newspapers are not as essential as they used to be. And there may never have been a time when covering state legislatures and local governments was more important than it will be in the coming years. With or without congressional legislation, more authority over welfare and Medicaid will shift to state governments. The Clinton administration is giving waivers of regulatory control to states that want to experiment in these two areas. And it seems certain, too, that the federal government will spend less on environment, leaving a vacuum for the states, if they choose to move into it. And this may be only the beginning of the shift of power from Washington to the state capitols.

Thus far, the signs as to whether the press will rise to the challenge are not good. Take a look at Washington for a clue. It has been important—imperative even—to provide detailed coverage of the U.S. Congress in the past fourteen months. Scores upon scores of vital issues have been joined. Profound change may be coming. Some of it has already happened. Yet only a handful of American newspapers—foremost among them the *New York Times*, I think—have covered it well and provided sufficient space for the coverage. What does this say about journalism and its responsibility to the public? What does it forecast for democracy?

The verdict is still out on Congress and what this portends for the future. But the trends for most newspapers are dismayingly clear. They are turning their backs on news and comprehensive coverage—the very things that made them community institutions and valuable properties in the first place. Editors and news staffs are becoming disenchanted, disheartened, and disillusioned. Recently, I had dinner with a friend of nearly thirty years. He is the top editor of an important metropolitan newspaper. Between the two of us we know a lot of top level editors. We reflected as we talked that very, very few of the editors we know really want to be editors of newspapers anymore. They are thinking of retirement, or of going into electronic journalism or, since they spend most of their time on budgets anyway, of becoming publishers or business managers. With the exception of a tiny handful of papers, the talk at the high levels of newspapers these days is of increasing profits, increasing corporate pressure, increasing responsibility to shareholders. Almost never is there talk of the financial commitment necessary to live up to our responsibilities to our communities and our nation. To talk of increasing coverage or staff on most newspapers now would be tantamount to confessing to lunacy. Such a tragedy because sound, readable, dependable news coverage is our future. Take care of our communities by covering them well and they will take care of us. Continue to neglect them and the future diminishes for us and our towns and cities.

But, alas, few newspaper corporations are getting this message. They are going the other way. I learn of new atrocities almost every time I attend a meeting of journalists or pick up a journalism publication. About a year ago, I read a story in the University of North Carolina *Journalist* that made what hair I have left stand on end.

The story told of efficiency consultants coming into the newsroom of the *Winston-Salem Journal*, once a fine independent daily now owned by the Media General corporation. The consultants developed a system for allotting the time allowed for each news assignment. Every story assignment carried a numerical and alphabetical classification.

Some examples, as cited by the *Journalist*:

"An A-1 story should be six inches or less. A reporter should use a press release and/or one or two `cooperative sources.' He or she should take 0.9 hours to do each story and should be able to produce 40 of these in a week."

"A B-3 story should come from a longer event and/or some uncooperative sources. It should be six inches to twelve inches, and the ideal reporter should churn out seven of them per week."

There are, of course, a hundred potential problems with such a system. Some of the best stories are unraveled by reporters like pulling at a loose string on a sweater. One phone call demands another, and then face-to-face interviews, and record checks, until finally the whole story develops. How could an editor possibly know in advance? Classification systems put handcuffs and headlocks on reporters. They defeat the spirit of determined inquiry and thoroughness. A paper with such a system is certain to under-inform its readers and become unnecessary to its community. Yet, such systems are almost the logical end result of the budgetary pressure corporations are putting on their newsrooms. Full-time staff equivalencies (FTEs in corporate parlance) are carefully rationed and steadily reduced on all but the tiniest fraction of newspapers.

You seldom hear of contingency budgets for major stories. Budgets are so tight, an editor must decide a year in advance how busy the coming news year will be. On the vast majority of papers you must cut back heavily on other coverage to handle a story like the Oklahoma City bombing that breaks without warning.

Newspaper managements may fool themselves, (but they do not fool serious readers), when they substitute fad-ism and gimmickry for substance And fad-ism and gimmickry are rampant in today's journalism. They manifests themselves in:

Riots of color that have no relationship to the news.

Sponsoring public meetings on public issues, rather than covering these same issues in depth.

Editors and publishers explaining themselves and their actions in weekly columns, rather than covering the news so well that the newspaper speaks for itself.

Charts and graphics that substitute for solid news coverage rather than amplifying and explaining that coverage.

Clustering and re-clustering reporters and editors, not because this enhances coverage, but because it might impress someone in the corporate hierarchy that you're abreast of the latest management trends, be they proven or unproven.

Fad-ism, standardization, and formula are especially common in chain newspapers, although most deny the obvious. Group-owned newspapers that are so obviously alike from town to town aren't likely to be meeting all their towns' coverage needs. Studies being done by David Coulson, professor of journalism at the University of Nevada, Reno, show a pronounced tendency to rely on corporate-wide wire services and news packages to the detriment of local news coverage. One study showed that more than half of all journalists interviewed (regardless of ownership) felt that their newspapers did not take strong editorial stands. And a close-up look at one newspaper, the Gannett-owned *Courier-Journal* in Louisville, showed that while overall news on the whole was up since Gannett acquired it ten years ago, much of the increase went to features and soft news. And wire service stories leaped by 76 percent in the ten years of Gannett ownership. While the number of local news stories had increased marginally, the average local story was significantly shorter. The bottom line: significantly less local news. What are the ramifications of remote ownership, bland content, formula, and fear of controversy on our newspapers, and our nation?

One way to gauge the changes wrought by chain ownership (and an almost industry-wide drive for profits at whatever cost) is to look at the American South. Few times in our history has there been such turmoil, angst, and bitterness as was experienced in the South during the civil rights era which extended from the Supreme Court's school desegregation decision in 1954 until about 1968 or 1969, roughly fifteen years.

Throughout much of the era, the central question was this: Would the white South remain so monolithic and adamantly against any form of racial integration that nothing could shake it, neither black activism nor Federal intervention? In the midst of this, a double-handful of southern newspapers—the great majority all but a couple of them locally, privately owned—stood firm on its editorial pages against bigotry and for compliance with the Supreme Court decision. In doing so, they made an incalculable difference. They showed the South was not monolithic. They served as a rallying point on racial issues for white moderates and progressives. A few even prodded reluctant presidents—with more effectiveness than a non-southern paper could ever muster.

Examining newspapers in the South at the time of the civil rights era in the 1950s and sixties, gives you an interesting perspective on the changes that have taken place. Of all the southern newspapers, the one that arguably demonstrated the most courage in covering school desegregation in detail in its news pages, and denouncing racism bigotry in its editorial pages was the *Arkansas Gazette* in Little Rock. When white mobs blocked blacks from entering Central High School, the *Gazette* urged a reluctant President Eisenhower, to enforce court desegregation rulings, else lawlessness would become rampant in Little Rock. Eisenhower ultimately acted, but the *Gazette's* bold act cost the paper heavily in circulation and advertising. The *Gazette* never wavered and rode out its financial crisis. Today, however, the paper no longer exists. It was swallowed up by one of America's largest chains, Gannett, which changed the character and tone of the paper, lost ground in the local newspaper war, and ultimately sold out to the underdog competitor, the *Arkansas Democrat*.

The most courageous newspaper in Mississippi throughout the civil rights era was the *Delta Democrat-Times* in Greenville, which was owned by the Hodding Carter family. After Carter wrote an article for *Look* magazine in which he exposed the dangers posed by white citizens councils, he was denounced as a liar in a resolution that passed in the Mississippi House of Representatives by a vote of 89 to 19. Carter reacted quickly in a front-page editorial, and totally in character. "If this charge were true, it would make me well-qualified to serve with that body. It is not true. So to even things up I herewith resolve by a vote of 1 to 0 that there are 89 liars in the State Legislature... those 89 character mobbers can go to hell collectively or singly and wait there until I back down. They needn't plan on returning."

Carter's paper. It is now owned by Freedom Newspapers, a chain based in the Orange County, California-based chain. And today it is the antithesis of what it was in the Carter years. "It does not support local civic and cultural groups the way the paper did when it was owned by Hodding Carter," Ann Waldron wrote in her biography of Carter. "And it never blasts injustice."

Greenville was different from most Delta towns because of the leadership provided by the *Delta Democrat-Times*, Waldron quoted Leroy Percy, a Greenville civic leader as saying, "I believe that more than 50 percent of the white people in town were glad to see the Carters go. Now all of them would be glad to see them back."

In Tennessee, the most courageous paper of the era was the *Nashville Tennessean*, which covered the local civil rights movement intensely while its competitor, the *Nashville Banner*, wavered between pretending the movement did not exist and believing it was a communist plot. Today, the *Tennessean* exists in blander form, one of the dailies owned by Gannett. On the other hand, Gannett owns the papers in Jackson, Mississippi. In the civil rights era, they were the most rabidly segregationist papers on the South. Today, under Gannett, they may veer toward formula journalism and blandness, but not toward bigotry.

Perhaps more than any single white man in the South, Ralph McGill, editor of the *Atlanta Constitution*, did the most in leading the South away from segregation. McGill came to believe that the South should abandon segregation, not simply because it was against the law of the land, but because it was the right and just thing to. He preached this in his seven-day-a-week, page-one column. Although the *Constitution* is owned by the same chain today, it no longer has a voice so prominent or unique as McGill's. But no other American newspaper has one either. Front-page opinion, however well-labeled, is passé.

In Richmond, the *News-Leader*, along with the Byrd political organization, led the state into an era of "massive resistance" and school closings. Ultimately the owner of the *News-Leader*, the Media General chain, expanded into North Carolina and bought the Winston-Salem newspapers, that stood steadfastly throughout the civil rights era for cool-headedness and compliance with the Supreme Court's desegregation decision. The Winston-Salem newsroom is, you may remember, the same newsroom that brought in consultants a couple of years ago and instituted a numerical and alphabetical classification system that determined how much time a reporter should spend on a story. Today, a new editor is trying hard to solve the many problems the system caused.

In Florida, the *St. Petersburg Times* was courageous and independently owned and remains courageous and independently owned today.

In Raleigh, North Carolina, the *News and Observer* stood firm in the civil rights era against closing schools to avoid desegregation. Jonathan Daniels, editor and part-owner, said it simply, but forcefully: Closing schools was something beyond secession from the Union; it was secession from civilization. In the past year the Daniels family sold the *News and Observer* to a chain, albeit one of the very best ones, McClatchy, which is based in Sacramento.

In Norfolk, Virginia, where schools were closed to evade desegregation, editor Lenoir Chambers and the editorial page of the *Virginian-Pilot*, was the one unwavering daily editorial voice against the State's policy of "massive resistance to racial integration." Today, the Norfolk newspaper company has evolved into a chain of daily newspapers, plus an important cable channel, and several local television stations. But Frank Batten, who backed Chambers in the civil rights era, is still at the helm of the organization.

While the picture is mixed, there has been more than enough deep-seated change to make you wonder whether newspapers could summon up the risk-taking and leadership to rise to a challenge as serious as the one in the 1950s and 1960s. And you might wonder to the same degree about newspapers in any region of the country. The overwhelming majority of them are distant from their ownership. And many are viewed by the corporations no differently than if they were chain retail outlets.

While quality varies, of course, from chain to chain and newspaper to newspaper, and there are good chain newspapers, and bad privately-owned ones, there is growing evidence that, on the whole, a significant number of communities are less well served in news coverage than they were under local ownership. Any major reversal in ownership patterns doesn't seem likely, but is there a solution short of that?

One answer is to monitor the chain's performance in the towns and cities in which they own newspapers and point it out when there are major patterns for good or bad in editorial leadership and in the coverage of local and state government and local institutions.

Who would do the monitoring? I would suggest the nation's journalism reviews, the *American Journalism Review*, the *Columbia Journalism Review* and *Nieman Reports*. The problem is that the two largest publications, *CJR* and *AJR*, seem to be teetering on the brink of extinction. And, the third, *Nieman Reports*, has a constant need for funding. They have problems in financing their present goals, which are far less ambitious and expensive than would be the detailed examination of the nation's largest newspaper chains one by one.

To examine even one chain would require an experienced reporter to spend at least one week in each of six or eight towns in which a chain operates. The reporter would examine how well the newspapers cover state and local government and public issues and institutions. And still more of them would be required for reporting at corporate headquarters and for writing. A thorough article would take three or four months and cost and average of $5,025 each in pay and expenses. This does not count newsprint and editing costs. Or the cost of printing extra copies for wider distribution. Perhaps twenty articles would be required over a two year period. At the end of the inquiry, a book should be published. In all, the project would cost between $750,000 to $2,000,000 spread over two to three years.

It is hard to imagine a project that a major foundation could fund, that would be more in the public interest. Ideally, one journalism review could examine newspaper groups while another examined television groups. But most newspaper foundation have been reluctant to provide major financial grants to the reviews. And non-newspaper foundations have yet to step forward. Yet, just one of them might, with a significant grant, point the way to greater corporate responsibility to the towns and cities with chain-owned papers.

In the end, communities cannot function well if they are not covered well. Seventy-five percent of the nation's 1,548 dailies are now in the hands of chains. And, thus, chains pipe the tune to which American journalism marches. Just four of the chains—Thomson, American, Gannett, and Donrey—own 21 percent of all of the country's dailies. And there are about fifteen more groups that are major players. To gauge just how little the public knows of newspaper groups, imagine yourself at a busy pedestrian intersection in a major city. Imagine how long you would have to wait and how many people you might have to interview, before you could find even one person who has heard of Thomson, or American, or Donrey. Yet more than 200 American towns and cities rely on these groups for their basic news coverage.

There will be no sense of accountability by some newspaper groups unless they are held up for public scrutiny. And who will would do this, unless the journalism reviews step in?

And today they, for the most part, regularly examine only the largest and best known of the nation's papers—the *New York Times*, the *Los Angeles Times*, the *Wall Street Journal*, and the *Washington Post*. And it is questionable how long they can afford to do even this. While no paper is without flaws and mistakes, if every paper took its obligations as seriously as these three four, the nation wouldn't have lasting problems with news coverage.

But this is not the case in town after town, city after city. State house coverage is increasingly under-covered even as it grows increasingly more important. Schools and hospitals are neglected, although they—especially hospitals—are undergoing major change. It is clear, painfully clear, that our newspaper chains bear watching. And the time to start is now.

Thomas Schatz

THE RETURN OF THE HOLLYWOOD STUDIO SYSTEM

Like death and taxes, the Hollywood studios seem to be forever with us. Paramount and Warner Bros. and the other entertainment behemoths who ruled Hollywood in its golden age of the 1930s and '40s now utterly dominate the so-called New Hollywood as well. These are scarcely the studios of old, however, given the structure and scope of the contemporary media marketplace and the changing form and function of the movies themselves. During Hollywood's classical era, the studios were geared to produce a singular commodity, the feature film, and to control a single culture industry. The New Hollywood studios, conversely, operate with an increasingly diversified, globalized "entertainment industry," and represent only one component of the vast media conglomerates which own them—media giants like Viacom, Sony, News Corp., and Time Warner. And while the driving force in the global entertainment industry is the motion picture, here, too, there are crucial differences from the classical era.

Over the past two decades—an unprecedented period of sustained financial success for the film industry—the studios have been geared to produce not simply films but "franchises," blockbuster-scale hits which can be systematically reproduced in a range of media forms. The ideal movie today is not only a box-office smash but a two-hour promotion for a multimedia product line, designed with the structure of both the parent company and the diversified media marketplace in mind. From *Jaws* to *Jurassic Park*, the New Hollywood has been driven (and shaped) by multipurpose entertainment machines which breed movie sequels and TV series, music videos and sound track albums, video games and theme park rides, graphic novels and comic books, and an endless array of licensed tie-ins and brand-name consumer products.

By way of brief example, consider *Jurassic Park*, the 1993 "summer blockbuster," which typifies the New Hollywood media franchise. The movie itself was a high-cost, effects-laden thriller and, of course, a monstrous hit. Created by Steven Spielberg and released by MCA-Universal, *Jurassic Park* cost $56 million to produce, with another $20 million spent on marketing (prints and advertising). It grossed a record $50.2 million in its opening weekend, reached $100 million in only nine days, and eventually grossed over $350 million in its domestic (United States and Canada) theatrical release. Its overseas box-office performance was even stronger, and together with its huge success on video cassette, pay-cable, and other ancillary markets, pushed the film's total revenues to well over a billion dollars.[1]

Jurassic Park, as an actual movie (in whatever delivery mode), represents only one facet of the franchise. According to an MCA merchandising executive, the film generated "the most comprehensive licensing program ever, both in terms of the volume of licenses and the huge number of promotional partners." The number of licensed product lines was approaching one thousand in the first year of release, and revenues from product tie-ins were expected to exceed the film's domestic box office. Among the more significant merchandising ventures in the United States was the Sega video-game version. MCA licensed the title and story line for *Jurassic Park* (adapted from Michael Crichton's best-seller) to a number of game manufacturers, and the most successful was the Sega version. Released in the United States on the same day as the movie, the Sega game also raced to record revenues, due largely to the fact that the player had the option of being a rampaging dinosaur rather than a fleeing human.[2]

Another record-setting reiteration was "Jurassic Park–The Ride," which opened in the summer of 1996 at Universal Studios Hollywood (the "studio tour" which has been redesigned as a theme park). The ride boosted attendance some 40 percent over the previous year, and it was touted as the primary reason for a general upswing in southern California tourism. On July 5, 1996, Universal set a one-day attendance record of forty-three thousand, which, at $30 per ticket, totals $1.3 million. Park-goers also can enjoy rides "based on" other films such as *King Kong, Back to the Future*, and *ET*, with the latter the most popular until the *Jurassic Park* spin-off. Spielberg designed the *ET*-inspired ride (as well as the *Jurassic Park* ride) at a cost of $110 million, some three times the cost of the original film. It debuted in 1991, a full decade after the release of the film, but in the midst of the theme-park frenzy which has steadily escalated since the mid-1980s.[3] Spielberg currently is working on the summer 1997 sequel to *Jurassic Park*, with the film and theme-park ride being designed and engineered simultaneously.[4]

As even these few examples indicate, "*Jurassic Park*, the franchise" comprises a profitable product line and a cultural commodity whose form directly reflects the structure of the media industry at large. It indicates, too, that the industry can scarcely be treated in terms of movies and video games and theme-park rides as separate entities or isolated media texts. Rather, they are related aspects or "iterations" of entertainment supertexts, multimedia narrative forms which can be expanded and exploited almost ad infinitum, given the size and diversity of today's globalized, diversified entertainment industry.

The essential UR-text within these media franchises is the Hollywood-produced blockbuster film and, thus, the key holding for today's media conglomerates is a film studio. Indeed, for Time Warner, and Disney, and the other media conglomerates, the studio's output tends to set the agenda for the entire company—which is scarcely surprising, given the enormous payoff of a successful franchise. And as the global entertainment industry has reached a certain equilibrium over the past decade, the production and calculated reformulation of these blockbuster films into multimedia franchises has become more systematic. In the process, the Hollywood "studio system" has been reformulated as well—albeit along very different lines from the system of old.

The Studio System in the "Old" Hollywood

The New Hollywood studio system is both an outgrowth of and a distinct departure from the system which emerged during the classical era. From the 1920s through the 1940s, the "studio system" referred to the factory-based mode of film production, and also, crucially, to the "vertical integration" of production with film distribution and exhibition. The Big Five "integrated major" studios—MGM, Warner Bros., 20th Century-Fox, Paramount, and RKO—ruled the industry not only because they produced top films, but because they collectively (and collusively) controlled the movie marketplace as well. The Big Five distributed their own films and ran their own theater chains. And while they owned only about one-sixth of the nation's movie theaters in the 1930s and '40s, this included most of the all-important "first-run" theaters—i.e., the downtown theater palaces that screened only top features, seated thousands of patrons, and generated well over half the total industry revenues.[5]

The major studios could not produce enough films to satisfy audience demand in an era when up to one hundred million persons per week went to the movies. Thus their output was supplemented by Universal, Columbia, and United Artists (UA), the "major minor" studios—major because they turned out A-class movies with top contract talent and had their own distribution arms; minor because they did not own their own theaters. The 1930s also saw the emergence of number of "minor" or "poverty row" studios like Monogram and Republic, which produced low-budget B-movies. These studios were outside the Hollywood power structure and only incidental to the studio system, since they did not produce A-class features and did not distribute their own films.

Vertical integration took hold during the 1920s and became standard operating procedure during the Depression and World War II, two national crises which led the government to sanction (or at least tolerate) the studios' monopolistic control of the film industry. This ensured the revenue flow and financial leverage for the studios to maintain their factory operations; it also enabled them to maintain a contract system, which kept crucial filmmaking talent at all levels, from top stars to stagehands, directly tied to the company.

In terms of movie product, the mainstay of the studio system was the A-class feature film, invariably a formulaic "star vehicle" with solid production values and a virtually guaranteed market. The studios turned out occasional big-budget "prestige" pictures, and they also cranked out a steady supply of low-cost formula quickies; in fact B-movies comprised up to half the total output of major studios like Fox and Warners in the 1930s. But the key commodity in classical Hollywood was the routine star-genre formulation—an MGM costume romance with Greta Garbo, a Warners' gangster saga with James Cagney or Edward G. Robinson, a Fox swashbuckler with Tyrone Power, and so on. Each studio's stable of contract stars were product lines unto themselves and, thus, the basis for each company's distinctive "house style." These trademark star-genre formulas gave each studio a means of stabilizing marketing and sales, of bringing efficiency and economy to top feature production, and of distinguishing the company's output from its competitors'.

Studio management in that vertically integrated system was a classic top-down affair, with the power emanating from the sales (i.e., distribution and exhibition) "end" of the business, centered in the home office in New York. Power passed from the top executives in New York to the "front office" of the studio on the West Coast. And while the New York office controlled the direction of capital (sales, marketing, budgeting, etc.), the studio executives, a continent away, oversaw production and thus controlled actual filmmaking. Indeed, it was not the so-called moguls or corporate CEO's in New York but these studio executives—men like Irving Thalberg, Darryl Zanuck, and David Selznick—who were the chief architects of Hollywood's golden age.

The Hollywood studio system flourished during World War II but then collapsed rather abruptly due to various factors, and three in particular. First and foremost was the Supreme Court's 1948 Paramount decree, an antitrust ruling which effectively disintegrated the studio system by forcing the studios to sell their theater chains. Second, was the emergence of television, which quickly transformed the American media landscape. The third factor involved wholesale changes in American lifestyles after the war—most notably via suburban migration and the so-called baby boom. With millions of returning servicemen marrying and starting families in the suburbs, "watching TV" soon replaced "going to the movies" as the nation's dominant form of habituated, mass-mediated narrative entertainment.

Although the Hollywood studios saw their audience fade and their revenues plummet in the 1950s, they managed to survive by radically changing the way they operated. In the process, they changed the very nature and structure of the movie industry. The studios recognized that without their theater chains, they lacked the cash flow to sustain their factory system and their contract talent. Thus they turned from production and exhibition to financing and distribution. The strategy here was to lease their studio facilities to the growing ranks of independent producers, and to provide a portion of a film's financing in return for the distribution rights. The studios also began cultivating a blockbuster mentality, realizing that releasing fewer, "bigger" films (many of them in wide-screen and Technicolor) was not only more practical and profitable in the 1950s movie marketplace, but also was an effective means of competing with TV.[6]

By the mid-1950s, this strategy clearly was paying off, with films like *The Ten Commandments* and *Around the World in 80 Days* redefining the profit potential and event status of Hollywood movies. At that point the studio powers decided to throw in with the television industry by selling or leasing their old films to TV syndicators, and also by producing "telefilm" series. Warners was the most aggressive in its television pursuits, and by 1961 was supplying over one-third of ABC's prime-time schedule. By then Hollywood was turning out far more hours of TV programming than feature films, having reactivated their B-movie production process to feed TV's voracious appetite for programming. In 1960, the networks started running feature films in prime time, and soon movies were on every evening of the week. Thus what once were studio "vaults" of virtually useless old movies were now "libraries" whose value increased with each passing year.[7]

Despite their growing rapport with the TV industry, however, the studios were seriously foundering in the late 1960s due to several key factors. One was the continued erosion of movie attendance, which had fallen to barely twenty million moviegoers per week (down from nearly one hundred million in the mid-1940s). Another factor was the nature and composition of that audience, i.e., the politically hip, disaffected youth who clearly preferred films like *Bonnie and Clyde* (1967), *Easy Rider* (1969), and *M*A*S*H* (1970) to the blockbusters that the studios were trying to sell. A third factor was a succession of big-budget flops, most of which were lavish musicals designed to replicate the huge success of *The Sound of Music* (1966). A fourth factor was the unprecedented surge in film imports which, by the late 1960s, represented almost two-thirds of the total U.S. releases.

The deepening movie industry recession left the studios ripe for takeover in the late 1960s, and in fact many were bought by large conglomerates—Warners by Kinney Corporation, Paramount by Gulf and Western, UA by Transamerica, and MGM by financier Kirk Kerkorian. At that point, the studios were valued more for their film libraries and TV series productions than for their filmmaking operations, and many observers felt that the studios—and the movie industry at large—were on the brink of complete collapse.

Into the New Hollywood

Reports of Hollywood's death were greatly exaggerated, however, and in the early 1970s, the industry began to rebound with films like

The Godfather, American Graffiti, The Sting, and *The Exorcist.* The real breakthrough came in 1975, spurred by a single film, *Jaws,* which both revived and redefined Hollywood's blockbuster tradition. *Jaws* was "pre-sold" via Peter Benchley's best-selling novel and "packaged" by a talent agency, ICM, which represented Benchley as well as the top talent involved in the movie, including director Steven Spielberg, who was among a new generation of film-makers (Francis Ford Coppola, George Lucas, et al.) who appealed not only to the hip, cine-literate, film-school generation, but to mainstream moviegoers as well. The film itself was a deft melding of genres—horrific revenge-of-nature film, supernatural thriller, slasher film, disaster film, buddy film, action-adventure thriller. And most fundamentally, *Jaws* was a chase film whose story was utterly conducive to Spielberg's visual technique, John Williams' pulsating score, and the wizardry of special effects experts.[8]

Jaws was targeted for a summer release (due mainly to the subject matter) in an era when most important films came out during the Christmas holidays. The producers mounted an unprecedented marketing campaign built around a massive network TV-ad blitz in the weeks before *Jaws'* nationwide release in over four hundred theaters. This "saturation" marketing campaign, although risky, proved eminently successful, creating the prototype for the "summer blockbuster." *Jaws* attracted thirty-eight million moviegoers in its first month of release enroute to a record box-office performance—the first movie ever to gross over $200 million and to return over $100 million in rentals to its distributor, Universal. The film also generated myriad commercial tie-ins, from toys and video games to sequels and soundtrack albums. Thus *Jaws* represented a movie franchise and product line very different from the star-genre formulas of the Old Hollywood; it was a veritable genre unto itself whose story could be reiterated in any number of media forms.

Opportunities for reiteration were about to increase due to enormous changes in media technology—changes crucial to the emergence of the New Hollywood which just happened to coincide with *Jaws'* release. The most important of these involved the emergence of the pay-cable and home video industries. In August 1975, an unknown cable outfit, HBO, became a nationwide cable movie channel via the launch of SATCOM I (the first geostationary commercial satellite). And, in October 1975, Sony introduced its Betamax video cassette recorder (VCR), thus launching the home-video industry. Other important developments in the mid-to-late 1970s included the explosive growth of the mall-based multiplex theater and the concurrent emergence of a new generation of moviegoer—younger and more conservative than the "youth market" of only a few years earlier, with a penchant for repeated viewings of their favorite films. Equally important was the rapid rise of two talent agencies created in the mid-70s, ICM and CAA, which specialized in packaging New Hollywood media franchises and which, along with the venerable William Morris Agency, grew even more powerful than the movie studios. The late 1970s also saw an upswing in defensive market tactics, notably an increase in sequels, series, reissues, and remakes.[9]

During the late 1970s, Hollywood's economic recovery was well underway, fueled by its revitalized blockbuster mentality. Total domestic grosses, which had reached $2 billion for the first time in 1975, surged 40 percent in only three years, with hits like *Rocky* (1976), *Star Wars, Close Encounters, Saturday Night Fever* (1977), *Grease* and *Superman* (1978) all doing record business.[10] While *Star Wars* was the top hit of the period, doing $127 million in rentals in 1977, and another $38 million as a reissue in 1978, *Saturday Night Fever* was a breakthrough as well, signaling the erosion of various industry barriers and the multimedia potential of movie hits, with its TV sitcom star (John Travolta), best-selling Bee Gees sound track, and "music movie" dynamic which helped spur both the "disco craze" of the late 1970s and the music video industry of the early 1980s.

In terms of both narrative structure and marketing, however, *Star Wars* was the ultimate New Hollywood commodity—a high-speed, hip-ironic, male action-adventure yarn whose central characters are essentially plot functions, with the plot itself eminently adaptable to ancillary media forms. The Lucas-designed "space epic" surpassed *Jaws* as Hollywood's all-time box-office hit, while securing the future for adolescent, by-the-numbers, male-action films. Indeed, from *Jaws* to *Star Wars* and onward into the 1980s, Hollywood's dominant products would become increasingly plot driven, increasingly visceral, kinetic, and fast-paced, increasingly "fantastic" and reliant on special effects, and increasingly targeted at younger audiences.

In an effort to broaden their appeal, however, these films also were strategically "open" to other formal and narrative possibilities. An important aspect of films like *Star Wars*, *Raiders of the Lost Ark*, *E.T.*, and their myriad successors, was the radical amalgamation of genre conventions and the elaborate play of cinematic references. *Star Wars*, as J. Hoberman writes, "pioneered the genre pastiche," and indeed the film's hell-bent narrative does careen from one genre-coded episode to another—from western to war film to vine-swinging adventure. This was reinforced by its nostalgic quality and evocations of old movie serials and TV series—references undoubtedly lost on younger viewers but relished by their cine-literate elders.[11]

Spielberg and Lucas were charter members of what Hoberman termed "Hollywood's delayed New Wave" whose "cult blockbusters" had elevated "the most vital and disreputable genres of their youth ... to cosmic heights." The two joined forces on *Raiders of the Lost Ark* (1981), establishing the billion-dollar Indiana Jones franchise. Whether working together or on their own projects, Lucas and Spielberg rewrote the box-office record books in the late 1970s and 1980s. With the release of their third Indiana Jones collaboration in 1989, the two could claim eight of the ten biggest hits in movie history, all of them surpassing $100 million in rentals. The auteur-entrepreneurs were, without question, the prime movers behind what *Variety*'s A.D. Murphy termed "the modern era of super-blockbuster films."[12]

The blockbuster films (and media franchises) of the late 1970s and the 1980s spurred not only the economic recovery of the movie industry but the emergence of the global, diversified entertainment industry as well. While Hollywood's domestic box-office revenues climbed at a steady pace (from $3 billion to over $5 billion in the course of the 1980s), its "ancillary" or "secondary" markets simply exploded. The principal growth areas throughout the 1980s were in home video and pay-cable, with the overseas markets (both theatrical and video) taking off later in the decade. During the 1990s, all of these markets have continued to grow at record levels, with the secondary markets steadily overwhelming Hollywood's once-sacrosanct domestic theatrical market. In the early 1980s, the domestic box office generated well over 50 percent of the studios' movie-related income; it now accounts for less than 15 percent. By 1995, foreign theatrical revenues surpassed Hollywood's domestic theatrical income, while the domestic home-video market generated over twice the revenues of the U.S. theatrical market.[13]

Thus the so-called ancillary markets, some of which were nonexistent in the early 1980s, now generate far more revenues for the studios than the domestic box office. But because all of these secondary markets are driven primarily by the Hollywood-produced blockbuster, the domestic theatrical market remains Hollywood's prime venue and primary focus. It is a movie's U.S. theatrical release—and, crucially, the accompanying marketing campaign—which serves as the "launch site" for its franchise development, establishing its value in all other media markets.[14]

Media Conglomeration in the New Hollywood

As it became evident that the Hollywood-produced blockbuster was the key commodity in an expanding global media marketplace, the status and value of the movie studios steadily grew. The result was a merger-and-acquisitions wave which began during the 1980s, with the movie studio as the central component in a new generation of media conglomerates. Beyond ownership of a major film studio, the basic requirements of these new media giants were deep pockets and "tight diversification." A media company today needs the financial muscle to have a reasonable chance to produce a blockbuster hit, and also the marketing muscle to make the most of a hit when it occurs.

Equally important, especially in expanding a hit film into a full-scale franchise, is tight diversification or "synergy"—i.e., bringing the studio into direct play with other media production entities and distribution outlets: TV series and video producers; broadcast networks and cable systems; music and recording companies; book, magazine, and newspaper publishers; video game and toy companies; theme parks and resorts; and electronics hardware manufacturers.[15]

Thus, the media conglomerates in the New Hollywood differ considerably from the studios of old and also from their more recent predecessors. In the Old Hollywood, the studios were all variations on the same corporate model; the parent company was primarily a theater chain, with its distribution system and movie factory as essential components. The parent companies of the 1960s and '70s, conversely, had little or nothing in common with one another or with their movie studios. Gulf & Western, Kinney Services, Transamerica, et al., had deep enough pockets, but they were too top-heavy and widely diversified to effectively exploit their media holdings. During the 1980s, those companies either sold off their media interests or "downsized" to achieve tighter diversification. Gulf & Western, for instance, siphoned off all but its media holdings in the course of the decade and, in 1989, changed its corporate name to Paramount Communications. Kinney created a media subsidiary in Warner Communications, which also downsized during the early 1980s, then steadily expanded until its epochal 1989 merger with Time Inc. Twentieth Century-Fox was bought (in 1985) by News Corp., thus becoming part of Rupert Murdoch's global media empire.

Other studios underwent less successful merger-acquisition alliances in the 1980s. UA collapsed in 1980 after a series of big-budget flops (most notably *Heaven's Gate*), and in 1981 merged with MGM. The once-glorious Metro-Goldwyn-Mayer was foundering itself at the time; in fact, it had ceased distribution altogether for much of the 1970s. In 1986, MGM sold off its film library to TBS (Turner Broadcasting System), and in 1989, was purchased—and essentially saved from bankruptcy—by the French company, Pathe Communications. Meanwhile Columbia Pictures, in the wake of its failed efforts to create an alliance with CBS and HBO in the early 1980s, was acquired by Coca-Cola in 1982 (the same year Columbia created its TriStar Pictures subsidiary). Coke and Columbia simply did not "fit," however, and in 1989, the studio was purchased, along with the highly successful CBS Records, by the Japanese media giant, Sony. The "hardware-software" alliance between Sony and Columbia, which was duplicated in 1990 when Matsushita acquired Universal-MCA, took synergy into another direction altogether.

The numerous media mergers and acquisitions in 1989 marked not only the end of the decade but a watershed of sorts for the Hollywood film industry. While the 1980s brought sustained economic recovery to the industry, it was also a period of considerable "churn" and uncertainty. Synergy was continually debated and redefined, affected by new technologies and new delivery systems, by an expanding and increasingly diversified media marketplace, by media deregulation, and by myriad other factors. But the principal of tight diversification steadily took hold, fueled by the output of blockbuster-scale hits and the cultivation of media franchises, and culminating in the veritable tidal wave of mergers and acquisitions in 1989—the biggest year ever for media-related deals. A total of 414 media deals were struck in 1989, worth over $42 billion, the most notable of which were the Time Warner merger ($14 billion) and Sony's buyout of Columbia and CBS Records ($5.4 billion).[16]

The wave subsided but then surged again in the mid-1990s, with 1995 setting yet another record with 644 media mergers totaling an astounding $70.8 billion. This included Viacom's buyout of Paramount in 1994 and Blockbuster Video in 1995 (for a total of $15.8 billion). Other 1995 transactions included Disney's purchase of Cap Cities/ABC ($19 billion), Time Warner's buyout of Turner Broadcasting ($7.3 billion), and Seagram's purchase of MCA/Universal ($5.7 billion). Also of note in 1995 was the Westinghouse buyout of CBS ($12.6 billion), as well as the creation of the DreamWorks SKG "studio" by Steven Spielberg, Jeffrey Katzenberg, and David Geffen.[17]

The merger wave undoubtedly will continue—an alliance between Westinghouse and a film studio seems all but inevitable, for instance—and the logic of tight diversification will continue to be refined in response to new technologies, new entertainment forms, changing consumer behavior, and an expanding global marketplace. But whatever their power and reach, the new media conglomerates can scarcely predict, let alone control, the vagaries of consumer behavior and the uncertainties of the media marketplace. And whatever the advantages of their size, in terms of economies of scale and maximization of profit on successful media ventures, these companies invariably face daunting problems coordinating their far-flung operations, integrating their disparate management cultures into a cohesive business strategy, and dealing with the shifting relations of power within and between their various units.

Despite the uncertainties and confusion, however, these new media conglomerates are enjoying record revenues and increasing hegemony over an expanding media marketplace. Indeed, just as the Big Five major film studios and the three TV networks once controlled their respective media industries, these conglomerates are now establishing their oligopoly power within the global entertainment arena. Disney, Time Warner, Viacom, News Corp., Sony, and Seagram's are among the most powerful media and entertainment companies in the world, and their success clearly is the result of tight diversification centering on the output of their film studios.[18] Indeed, the status of the film studio for these media giants is emphatically underscored by the current obsession with "branding"—i.e., the relentless marketing of the studio's name, its corporate logo, and its trademark stars and media figures. And increasingly, the studio's filmed entertainment division tends to set the agenda for the entire corporation, including the parent conglomerate.

With the studios' collective return to power, and especially since the 1989 merger wave, the Hollywood studio system itself has undergone a steady, seemingly inexorable, rebirth. Simply stated, the 1990s has witnessed the regeneration of the studio system, albeit reconfigured to the economic and industrial contours of the New Hollywood. Rather than a return to the system of old, in other words, this rebirth has involved a seismic paradigm shift.

Disney, Warners, and the New Hollywood Studio System

The most successful and powerful of the studios over the past decade and the defining entities in the revitalized studio system have been Disney and Warner Bros. The two have utterly dominated the motion picture industry, finishing first and second at the box office every year since 1991 while sharing 35 to 40 percent of the market. Meanwhile their parent companies (The Walt Disney Company and Time Warner, Inc.) have become the two leading global media powers in terms of revenues and volume of business.[19] In fact, the recent Disney merger with Cap Cities/ABC and the Time Warner merger with Turner (both of which were initiated in 1995, withstood various legal challenges, and were approved by the FCC in 1996) put the two in a class by themselves among media conglomerates.

The emergence of Warner Bros. and Disney as a veritable media duopoly has been propelled by the strategic expansion of their parent companies over the past decade. In both cases, this "upsizing" has been keyed, on the one hand, to the film studio and its signature franchises, and on the other, to the rapid changes in the global entertainment industry. The two parent companies are models of tight diversification as well, in terms of both vertical and horizontal integration. Warner and Disney have integrated vertically by complementing film production with distribution-exhibition "pipelines" to consumers. And they have integrated horizontally by developing an array of entertainment subsidiaries, from music to print media to theme parks, to augment their studio output and, when appropriate, to better exploit their franchise operations.

Interestingly enough, the recent Disney-ABC and Time Warner-Turner mergers have brought the two companies into fairly close alignment structurally, even though the earlier expansion process for each company has been quite different. Disney, until 1995, expanded primarily from within, either by upsizing an established division (adding theme parks in Tokyo and Paris, for instance, or expanding film production via Touchstone and Hollywood Pictures), or else by developing a new venture on its own (most notably its chain of retail stores). The 1993 purchase of Miramax for the relatively modest sum of $65 million indicated Disney's willingness to go the merger acquisition route, but no one in the industry was expecting the mammoth ABC deal.[20] The $19 billion purchase of Cap Cities/ABC was a necessary move, however, because it gave Disney key components it simply could not cultivate from within. Chief among these were broadcast and cable outlets, including the ABC network with its 225 affiliates and eight "O&O's" (owned-and-operated stations), a nationwide radio network (with twenty-one stations), as well as the ESPN, A&E, and Lifetime cable networks. ABC also had developed video and cable interests overseas, with coproduction deals and programming alliances in England, Germany, France, Japan, and elsewhere.[21]

While the primary benefits of the merger involved vertical integration, it also enhanced Disney's horizontal expansion, especially in terms of Cap Cities' magazine and newspaper publishing divisions. Thus the makeup of the newly merged Disney-ABC empire, as indicated by the proportionate revenues its divisions, was as follows[22]:

broadcasting, cable	32%
filmed entertainment	29
theme parks, resorts	21
consumer products	11
publishing	7

Whereas Disney grew mainly from within until its epochal ABC merger, Warners' development throughout the 1980s and '90s simply extended a long history of mergers and acquisitions. Warner Communications had entered the 1980s, in fact, in the throes of an ill-fated, high-stakes alliance with the video game and home computer giant, Atari. Warner soon abandoned these pursuits, while it enjoyed more effective acquisitions with Geffen Records and with

Lorimar, the telefilm producer. At the point of its 1989 merger with Time, Warner was on a remarkable roll. The studio was number one in film rentals, thanks largely to *Batman*, and had been among the top three for seven straight years. The Warner-Lorimar telefilm arm had eighteen series on prime-time TV. Warner Bros. International and Warner Home Video were enjoying steady growth, and the Warner Music Group boasted the world's largest and most profitable music recording, publishing, and distribution setup.[23]

The Time Warner alliance created a remarkably well-balanced media conglomerate, with the proportionate revenues of its main divisions as follows:

magazines	24%
filmed entertainment	17
cable television	15.5
music recording, publishing	15
programming (HBO)	15
books	13.5

But while it was envisioned as an ideal merging of publishing and entertainment, the greatest benefits came via the vertical integration of Warners' media production and Time's video and cable interests— i.e., HBO and Cinemax, a stake in TBS, and the ATC cable system with its 4.4 million subscribers.[24]

Time Warner steadily expanded during the 1990s, most notably via its half-stake in the Six Flags theme parks and its buyout of Turner's TBS. The 1995 TBS deal was crucial on several counts: First, the cable and broadcast networks (CNN, TNT, superstation TBS, et al.) gave Time Warner a guaranteed outlet for its media products. Second, the addition of several "smaller" film studios (Castle Rock, New Line, Fine Line) would augment Warner Bros.' mainstream films with more specialized fare. Third, TBS' massive film and TV series holdings gave Time Warner the largest library in existence—including movie holdings of over 3,500 titles. And fourth, the Time Warner news division now enjoyed both cable and print components. The TBS deal also gave Time Warner several Atlanta-based pro sports franchises, although the value of these holdings to Time Warner remains to be seen.[25]

After the merger, Time Warner began operating with three primary divisions: entertainment, news, and telecommunications. The longtime studio management team of Robert Daly and Terry Semel ruled the entertainment division and functioned as seconds-in-command to CEO and Chairman Gerald Levin. They enjoyed more authority, in fact, than even Ted Turner, who as vice-chairman and majority stockholder (with 11 percent of the voting stock) was the closest thing to an "owner" and "mogul" at Time Warner, and who had a history of hands-on management at TBS.[26]

The Daly-Semel situation at Time Warner points up two crucial aspects of the resurgent studio system, both of which were evident at Disney as well. The first was the centrality of the movie studio and filmed entertainment division to the overall operation and market strategy of the company; the second was the importance of stable management to the studio's success. At both Time Warner and Disney, filmed entertainment has far out-paced the other divisions in terms of growth and performance, becoming the shaping force in the company's development. At Warner, revenues from filmed entertainment (including both movies and telefilm) grew from $1.2 billion in 1985 to $5 billion in 1995; after the merger with Time, film revenues grew from roughly one-sixth to over one-third of the company's total income by 1996.[27] The growth of Disney's filmed entertainment division was even more pronounced. In 1986, studio revenues were $512 million, only 20 percent of Disney's total. In the fiscal year prior to the 1995 Cap Cities merger, film studio revenues were $4.7 billion, nearly one-half of Disney's $10.06 billion total.[28]

This growth in filmed entertainment was orchestrated at both companies by a stable, capable management team—by Daly and Semel under CEO Steven Ross at Warners, and by Michael Eisner and Jeffrey Katzenberg under Frank Wells at Disney. Moreover, these studio executives were able to operate with little interference from a hands-on owner-mogul (like Rupert Murdoch of News Corp. or Sumner Redstone of Viacom). *Variety* editor Peter Bart, an astute analyst and former studio executive, has noted the "Napoleonic" complex displayed by the new breed of media mogul—a key factor in the heavy turnover of studio management executives at Fox, Paramount, and elsewhere.[29]

Daly and Semel, who have run Warner Bros. since the late 1970s, remain firmly ensconced at the studio despite the shakeups after Ross's death (and the ascent of Gerald Levin) in 1994, and the Turner deal in 1995. The role of Turner himself as vice-chairman of Time Warner remains uncertain, although he seems willing to maintain a hands-off rapport with the film studio and the entertainment division. The situation at Disney, meanwhile, is far more uncertain and, in fact, has been quite volatile since Wells' sudden, unexpected death (in a helicopter crash) in 1994. Eisner took over Wells' role as CEO but then balked at promoting Katzenberg—who promptly left to create Dreamworks SKG with Steven Spielberg and David Geffen. Meanwhile, Eisner hired Michael Ovitz, cofounder and CEO of Creative Artists Agency (CAA), as his second-in-command, and promoted Joe Roth to studio chief. Ovitz's move from CAA to Disney sent yet another signal of the changing power structure in Hollywood, as the control of film production shifted from the stars and talent agencies back to the studios. But Ovitz lasted only a year at Disney, leaving in late 1996 due to conflicts with Eisner, who began showing symptoms of a Napoleonic complex of his own atop the Disney-ABC empire.[30]

Franchise Fever: "The whole machine of the company"

Regardless of who manages the major film studios, he or she necessarily will pursue the now-dominant franchise mentality—particularly at Disney and Warner Bros., whose enormous success in the 1990s has come via the blockbuster-scale film and the resultant media franchise. The trademark Disney franchise, of course, is the animated feature—although this was decidedly not the case when "Team Disney" (Wells, Eisenberg, Katzenberg, et al.) took over in the mid-1980s. At the time, Disney had not had an animated hit in decades, and the only one in active production was *The Black Cauldron*, its most expensive and ambitious cartoon feature since *Sleeping Beauty* in 1959. While the studio turned out a number of successful live-action films in 1986, notably *Down and Out in Beverly Hills, Ruthless People*, and *The Color of Money*, the prime objective of Team Disney, and particularly Jeffrey Katzenberg, was to reestablish the animated feature as Disney's signature product.[31]

Over the next few years, the animation unit was steadily expanded from 150 to over 700 employees and by 1988, there were clear indications that Katzenberg was turning things around: *Who Framed Roger Rabbit?*, a breakthrough amalgam of animation and live action; *The Fox and the Hound*, the first fully-animated feature under the new regime; and the successful reissue of *Bambi*, originally released in 1942.[32] Disney's first animated hit was *The Little Mermaid* in 1989, and from that point on Disney has enjoyed one blockbuster after another with both its new films and its reissues: *The Jungle Book* (reissue, 1990), *Beauty and the Beast* (1991), *Aladdin* (1992), *Snow White and the Seven Dwarfs* (reissue, 1993), *The Lion King* (1994), *Pocahontas* (1995), *Toy Story* (1995), and *The Hunchback of Notre Dame* (1996).

Without question, these animated features spurred the Disney surge. As *Variety* reported in 1993: "While filmed entertainment accounts for approximately 35 percent of Disney's total operating income, Chairman Michael Eisner readily acknowledges that the animation division drives the entire company—providing rides for theme parks, products for the merchandising division, even inspiration for the logo for Disney's new hockey team, the Mighty Ducks."[33] Disney closed out 1996 with yet another variation on its animation franchise strategy with a live-action version of its 1961 animated feature, *101 Dalmations*—a huge box-office hit which pushed the total number of Dalmation-related product lines to a staggering seventeen thousand.[34]

Warner Bros., meanwhile, specialized in the lone-hero, action-adventure formula—most notably Clint Eastwood and Mel Gibson vehicles, whose long association with the studio renders them the New Hollywood equivalent to the "contract stars" of old.[35] Both have been associated with familiar Warners series—Eastwood with the Dirty

Harry films and Westerns, Gibson with the Lethal Weapon films—and have become veritable franchises unto themselves. These have been vital to Warner's success, but its signature franchise of the 1990s has been its *Batman* series. As Corey Brown noted in a recent *Premiere* profile: "Warners is the studio that *Batman* built. Not only did the $250 million grosser create the billion-dollar *Batman* industry, it inspired Semel and Daly to create the worldwide chain of Warner retail stores, as well as give a boost to the long-dormant animation division." In that article, Semel is quoted as saying, "The first picture that blew us out was *Batman....* It was the first time we utilized the whole machine of the company. The marketing, the tie-ins, the merchandising, the international."[36]

The success of Time Warner's *Batman* franchise is virtually incalculable, given the range of related products generated since the 1989 series regeneration. Besides its performance as a film—$250 million domestic box office, $160 million overseas, $180 million in video cassette sales, etc.—*Batman* was "a milestone in entertainment licensing and merchandising," according to *Variety*, generating a reported half-billion dollars in worldwide merchandising. The sequel, *Batman Returns* (1992), was a solid box-office hit ($163 million domestic; $120 million foreign), but a severe disappointment in terms of merchandising. Its dismal commercial afterlife was attributed to several factors: the darkness of the story (and Tim Burton's direction), Michael Keaton's grimly heroic Batman, and the manic intensity of the film's antagonists (especially Danny Devito's "Penguin"). Warners decided to "lighten up" the next series installment, *Batman Forever* (1995), replacing Burton with director Joel Schumacher and Keaton with Val Kilmer, and centering the story—and the advertising campaign—on rising comic star Jim Carrey as the Riddler, a more upbeat, engaging nemesis.[37]

The *Batman* series redesign was an obvious success. *Batman Forever* grossed $185 million in the U.S. and another $150 million overseas, and was a merchandising bonanza. According to Dan Romanelli, head of Warners' consumer products division, *Batman*

Forever has generated over one billion dollars in licensing and tie-ins. The *New York Times* reported in 1996 that *Batman* merchandise had earned over $4 billion.[38] This did not include the *Batman*-related theme-park rides, which represent yet another kind of tie-in. In May 1992, Six Flags (half-owned by Time Warner) introduced "Batman—The Ride" to coincide with the release of *Batman Returns*, and it introduced "Joker's Revenge" in the summer of 1996 to coincide with *Batman Forever.*[39]

The success of *Batman* in home video well indicates the importance of the movie "library" in the age of the VCR. Here, too, Warner and Disney have dominated the field—albeit with markedly different strategies. While *Batman* set an industry standard as a "sell-through" (versus rental) videotape with just over ten million units sold, it was actually an exception for Warners, which has preferred rental over sell-through—thus maintaining the value of its own library rather than the "home libraries" of consumers. Disney pioneered the sell-through strategy, retailing its animated franchise hits on cassette via its Buena Vista Home Video arm, with both reissues and new titles breaking one sales record after another. In 1993, for instance, *Aladdin* sold 10.6 million copies in only its first three days, enroute to a record total of 24 million; and in 1994 the reissued *Snow White and the Seven Dwarfs* surpassed that total, generating over $300 million in home-video revenues.[40]

Time Warner has continued to concentrate on its own library, with the TBS merger adding over 3,500 feature film titles to Warner Bros. holdings of some 1100 titles.[41] Among the films in its library, of course, are Warner Bros.' vintage Looney Tunes shorts with Bugs Bunny, Daffy Duck, et al. These have enjoyed spectacular and surprising success in syndication, and their shelf life may render them the most valuable of Time Warner's franchises. According to Consumer Products Chief Romanelli, total revenues of merchandise related to Warner Bros.' Looney Tunes figures reached an astounding $3.5 billion in 1996.[42]

This underscores yet again the importance of merchandising and product licensing, which may be the single most significant current (and future) development in the New Hollywood. In 1994, worldwide retail sales of all licensed products surpassed $100 billion for the first time ever; roughly 70 percent of that business was done in the U.S. In 1995, sales of entertainment-related merchandise was an estimated $28 billion. Besides producing these enormous revenues, merchandising and product licensing benefit the media conglomerates in other important ways as well. They forge brand-name identity and awareness, with thousands of licensed products "branding" not only a particular film or franchise but the studio itself. Tie-ins can spur more rapid and efficient expansion into foreign markets, and also can lead to joint ventures with other high-visibility corporations, from fast-food giants to video game and toy manufacturers. Here, the financial as well as promotional benefits can be substantial. Burger King's record deal with Disney for *Toy Story* in 1995, for instance, was worth an estimated $45 million in ads and other promotions.[43]

Disney has long been the industry leader in the licensing and merchandising arena, and that success encouraged Eisner to develop another aspect the consumer products division—namely, the Disney-owned chain of retail stores. This move is scarcely surprising, considering both the economic and synergy-related benefits of the studios selling their own entertainment-related products. Disney initiated this effort in 1987, opening a retail store in Glendale, California. The store was an instant success, and by 1990, Disney had added over fifty retail outlets, thus openly competing with its licensees for what *Business Week* described as a $2 billion U.S. market for "Disney knick-knacks."[44] Disney has continued to globally expand its retail chain at a remarkable rate—including one hundred new U.S. outlets in 1995 and a 30,000-square-foot flagship store in New York City in 1996.[45]

Warner Bros. has been the most aggressive among the other studios in following Disney's lead, and it, too, has enjoyed huge success in the retail arena. After creating a consumer products division in 1987, Warners launched its own retail chain in 1991. The total number of Warner Bros. stores surpassed 150 in 1996; and its New York flagship store (on Fifth Avenue) also underwent massive expansion to nine floors and 75,000 square feet. That expansion was demanded by the tremendous volume of business—an average of some twenty thousand shoppers per day—and by other factors as well, particularly the TBS deal which brought Hanna-Barbera Productions and its animated stars (Huckleberry Hound, The Flintstones, et al.) into the Time Warner fold. By now, the other media powers are quickly following suit. Viacom-Paramount is planning its own flagship store in Chicago, for example, and even the television networks have announced similar ventures.[46]

The importance of the studios' retail chains and consumer products divisions can scarcely be overstated. The ultimate objective here is to blur or erase altogether the distinction between shopping and entertainment—to create, in *Variety*'s terms, "theme-park-style gift shops." Scarcely "shops" in any conventional sense, these entertainment-related facilities will contain movie theaters of various kinds (including IMAX), interactive arcades, simulated theme-park rides, virtual reality playscapes, and, of course, retail stores.[47] Disney and Warner are both at a tremendous advantage here, due not only to their substantial lead over the competition but also to the sheer number (and obvious durability) of their franchises—especially the presold, animation-based stories and figures which tend to have the widest demographic appeal.

Whatever their franchise inventory, however, Disney and Warner Bros., and the other studios must continually renew their product lines via new blockbuster-scale hits—an ever more costly venture as the "risk-reward" quotient steadily increases. Thus, the studios are producing more (and more expensive) films every year, and spending more to market those films as well. In 1990, the average cost of 169 major studio productions was $28.8 million, with another $11.6 million spent on marketing (prints and advertising). In 1995, the average cost on 212 productions was $36.4 million, plus $17.7 for marketing, pushing the total cost per feature over $50 million for the first time ever. The most significant increase was in "ad buys," which totaled $1.94 billion for all releases in 1995—up 107 percent over 1990.[48]

Disney far out-paced the other studios in ad buys, spending $432.6 million on film-related ads in 1995—over 60 percent more than its nearest competitors, Sony and Warner (both at about $265 million).[49] Disney was widely criticized for this seeming extravagance, but studio head Joe Roth dismissed such criticism as "narrow thinking" in an interview with *Variety*'s Peter Bart. "You can't think of advertising in terms of domestic theatrical films alone," said Roth. "A major studio spends to stimulate all of the revenue streams, from merchandising to video to theme parks.... To not see the strategy of release dates and ways to create event advertising as weapons sometimes equal to the movie idea is missing the point."[50]

Conclusion

Roth's view seems reasonable enough, given the structure and economic imperatives of the New Hollywood. It also serves as a reply of sorts to the now-legendary "Katzenberg memo" issued by Roth's predecessor. In January 1991, in an internal memorandum to Eisner, Wells, and other top Disney executives, Jeffrey Katzenberg lamented the "tidal wave of runaway costs and mindless competition" and "the 'blockbuster mentality' that has gripped our industry." Successful films, he said, are "primarily based on two elements—*a good story, well executed*." And the bottom line was conceptual, not commercial: "We must not be distracted from one fundamental concept: the idea is king."[51] This was a far cry, indeed, from Roth's notion of marketing strategies "as weapons sometimes equal to the movie idea."

Katzenberg's memo was motivated by the cost overruns and relatively weak box office of *Dick Tracy*, the 1990 Disney film that cost $46 million to produce and an astounding $55 million to market and release.[52] It was motivated, too, by the huge success of Disney's *Pretty Woman*, which along with *Home Alone* and *Ghost*, dominated the box office in 1990, outgrossing (and far outearning) such calculated blockbusters as *Total Recall, Die Hard, The Hunt for Red October, Back to the Future III, Another 48 Hours*, and *Days of Thunder*. Bolstered by this apparent reversal of box-office fortunes and perhaps a dose of New Year's resolve, Katzenberg advocated a return to films like *Pretty Woman*, "the kind of modest, story-driven movie we tended to make in our salad days."[53]

The success of those more "modest" 1990 films turned out to be an aberration, however. The movie marketplace since then has been ruled by high-cost blockbusters and blatant franchise fare, with Disney's animated features like *Aladdin* and *The Lion King* (both number one box office films in their respective release years) managing to strike a balance between the crassly commercial and the well-crafted classical product. Katzenberg may have seen these as endorsing the views in his 1991 memo but, in fact, the kind of tight, well-crafted story he espoused is no longer viable in an industry whose films are designed to spawn product lines and theme-park rides. Katzenberg's final animation project before leaving Disney is a case in point. *The Hunchback of Notre Dame* (1996) transformed Victor Hugo's dark tale into an upbeat, user-friendly musical, and its horrific hero into an endearing and eminently marketable cartoon figure.

As the blockbuster mentality and franchise fever steadily intensify, distinctions between film culture and consumer culture are steadily being eradicated. That is precisely the objective of the studios and their parent companies, of course, and is endemic to a culture industry which always has subordinated craft to commerce. Indeed, the imminent convergence of movie theater, theme park, and retail store is the New Hollywood equivalent of the studio-owned movie palace of old—i.e., the site at which "the whole machine of the company," in all its integrated glory, can be most efficiently and profitably exploited.

This presupposes the ongoing appeal of movies themselves, and, in fact, the Hollywood-produced motion picture does continue to attract audiences—in ever increasing numbers, in fact, when the international marketplace is taken into account. Moreover, Hollywood's worldwide market provides yet another rationale for by-the-numbers chase films and tales of adolescent fancy, which tend to sell so well overseas. And in the view of Hollywood's consummate auteur-entrepreneur, Steven Spielberg, the blockbuster is less a matter of dumbing down the classical narrative than of endowing it with the simplicity and essence of myth. Commenting on the global success of *Jurassic Park*, Spielberg has said: "Once upon a time it was a small gathering of people around a fire listening to the storyteller with his tales of magic and fantasy. And now it's the whole world.... That's what has thrilled me most about the 'Jurassic Park' phenomenon. It's not 'domination' by American cinema. It's just the magic of storytelling, and it unites the world."[54]

In terms of both storytelling and myth-making, Speilberg's point is well taken. *Jurassic Park* may be lacking in terms of character and plot development and in thematic complexity, but it is a wondrously well-crafted movie—a visceral theme-park ride (in fact, a preview of the ride itself) and a dazzling display of digital effects. It is scarcely on a par with *Jaws*, the New Hollywood's UR-Blockbuster; but as template for the 1990s global franchise, *Jurassic Park* is a masterwork. Equally important is its elemental treatment of nature and technology, an opposition which operates not only on the levels of style and story but in the generation of the images themselves. Thus the notion that Hollywood's traditional myth-making function now operates on a global scale, particularly in the blockbuster and franchise fare with its exponential growth rate overseas. Perhaps the clearest signal of the "end of history" and triumph of capitalism in the post-Cold War era is the steady diffusion of Hollywood-produced entertainment and the seemingly inexorable Disney-fixation of global culture.

Whether the media conglomerates can continue to expand their far-flung operations and maintain their synergies on a worldwide scale, however, is open to question. "To survive in the '90s," writes Peter Bart, "a company must mobilize a vast array of global brands to command both content and distribution. Indeed, such an enterprise must be more than a company—it must be a virtual nation-state."[55] Bart fears that the conflicting agendas of their various sectors and their sheer size will "immobilize" these companies, which is a serious concern regarding markets like China and India. But the media conglomerates are aggressively pursuing these markets just the same, given the size and thus the financial rewards at stake.

As the media empires continue to extend their global reach, they also are considering ways to tighten diversification and thus to function more economically and efficiently. At present, the governing wisdom is that the media conglomerates could streamline operations and reduce debt by siphoning off their print and publishing divisions. Seagram's, Universal-MCA's parent company, recently followed this course by selling Putnam Berkley, its publishing subdivision. Commenting on the sale, Seagram's Vice Chairman Bob Matschullat explained that "we didn't see substantial synergies" between MCA and Putnam. But other companies have enjoyed tremendous success with their film-publishing tie-ins—Viacom's Simon & Schuster with an entire division devoted to Star Trek, for instance, and News Corp.'s recent success with novels based on Fox-TV's *X-Files* series.[56]

Interestingly enough, the most successful movie-related publishing franchise is Bantam Books' *Star Wars* series, developed in an alliance not with Fox (which produced and released the films) but with Lucasfilm Licensing. In one of the savviest moves in media history, George Lucas waived a half-million-dollar bonus on *Star Wars* in 1977 in exchange for the merchandising and sequel rights to the film. While costing Fox untold billions of dollars, this deal provided Lucas with the seed money to create his own media empire (Lucasfilm Limited, Industrial Light and Magic, et al.), and to develop the franchise without the resources or the constraints of a parent company. It also underscored the importance of "top talent" in the creation and cultivation of both hit movies and media franchises.[57]

Controlling top talent—particularly directors, stars, writers, composers, and producers—has been a key objective of the rejuvenated studios in recent years, in an effort to revive the "contract system" which was so essential to the Old Hollywood studio system. This has been less than successful, however, in an era when film stars, directors, and other media celebrities can become veritable franchises unto themselves, while their agents and attorneys arrange strategic alliances (rather than binding contracts) with the studios. The success of Lucasfilms' new *Star Wars* trilogy, slated for release in 1998-2000, and the fate of Spielberg's new Dreamworks setup should provide a good indication of whether top talent can maintain their relative autonomy and financial leverage in the current climate of concentrated media power and renewed oligopoly.

This concentration of power raises other concerns as well—concerns which far outweigh the status of artists who have long since accepted the commercial exigencies of the contemporary entertainment industry. Hollywood's top talent have done the bidding of the blockbuster-driven, franchise-fevered studios all too well, and consequently the filmed entertainment divisions are dictating and defining not only the agendas of the media conglomerates but the very nature and shape of media expression. Well beyond the convergence of moviegoing and shopping, we are witnessing the confluence of entertainment, information, and advertising at a rapid and alarming rate.

In an era when information is power but is also packaged as "consumer entertainment," the concentration of media control in the hands of a conglomerate cartel grows increasingly worrisome, due less to any fears of the political clout of the new media moguls and their communication empires, than to their blithe disregard for the political—i.e., for the free and open flow of information so crucial to social and economic justice. In a global media culture unified by rituals of entertainment and patterns of consumption, those who cannot afford to consume are likely to be factored out of the cultural and political equation. And those social and political issues which cannot be rendered in sufficiently "entertaining" terms are likely to be either ignored or relegated to the far reaches of the 500-channel universe.

The likelihood of any international regulation of these media giants or of the global entertainment marketplace at large seems highly remote, especially in light of the difficulties in dealing with international copyright and intellectual property issues. In the United States, both the FCC and Congress have indicated a willingness to deregulate the media industry (most recently in the revised Communications Act), thus enabling Viacom, Disney, Time Warner, et al., to compete in the high-stakes global media marketplace with precious few constraints. While this bodes well for these companies and for bedazzled media consumers, the outlook regarding the aesthetics of cinema or the enlightenment of the audience is rather dismal. Indeed, the continued growth and ever expanding power of these media giants will test, perhaps more than anything else, whether these communications empires and the moguls who control them have any real sense of moral, political, and cultural responsibility to the global community which their companies are both creating and exploiting.

Notes

1   *Variety*, June 28, 1993, 5; *Variety* Sept 21, 1993, 7–8; *Variety* Oct 18, 1993, 1; *Variety*, Oct 17-23, 1994. By late 1994, according to *Variety*, *Jurassic Park* had grossed $356.5 million in the domestic (U.S. and Canada) theatrical market, and $555.8 million in theaters overseas. Here and throughout this essay, I refer to "*rentals*" (or "rental receipts") and also to "gross revenues" (or "box-office revenues"). This is a crucial distinction, since the gross revenues indicate the amount of money actually spent at the box office, whereas rental receipts refer, as *Variety* puts it, to "actual amounts received by the distributor"—i.e., the moneys returned by theaters to the company (usually a "studio") that released the movie. Unless otherwise indicated, both the rentals and gross revenues involve only the "domestic" market—i.e., theatrical release in the U.S. and Canada. All of the references to box-office performance and rental receipts in this articles are taken from *Variety*, most of them from its most recent (May 9-15, 1994; 40–52) survey of "All-Time Film Rental Champs," which includes all motion pictures returning at least $4 million in rentals. Because this survey is continually updated, the totals include re-issues and thus may be considerably higher than the rentals from initial release. In these cases I try use figures from earlier *Variety* surveys for purposes of accuracy.

2   "Special Report" on the merchandising of *Jurassic Park*, *Variety*, Dec 27, 1993, 57+.

3 Aaron Latham, "At Universal, It's Only a Movie," *The New YorkTimes*, Sept 29, 1996, 14+ (Sunday Arts & Leisure).

4 *Variety*, Apr 29–May 5, 1996, 1+.

5 Recent studies of "classical" Hollywood and the "studio system" include *The Classical Hollywood Cinema: Film Style and Mode of Production to 1960*, David Bordwell, Janet Staiger, and Kristin Thompson (New York: Columbia University Press, 1985); Douglas Gomery, *The Hollywood Studio System* (New York: St. Martin, 1986); and Thomas Schatz, *The Genius of the System: Hollywood Filmmaking in the Studio Era*, (New York: Pantheon, 1988).

6 For a thorough treatment of Hollywood's postwar transformation through the 1980s, see *Hollywood in the Age of Television*, Tino Balio, ed. (Boston: Unwin Hyman, 1990). See also Christopher Anderson, *Hollywood TV* (Austin: University of Texas Press, 1994).

7 Tino Balio, "Introduction to Part II," and William Lafferty, "Feature Films on Prime-Time Television" in Balio, ed. *Hollywood in the Age of Television*.

8 Thomas Schatz, "The New Hollywood," in *Film Theory Goes to the Movies*, Jim Collins, et al., eds. (New York: Routledge, 1993), 8-36.

9 On home video and pay-cable, see Michelle Hilmes, "Breaking the Broadcast Bottleneck," and Bruce A. Austin, "Home Video: The Second-Run 'Theater' of the 1990s," in Balio, ed. *Hollywood in the Age of Television*. On sequels and reissues, see Joseph R. Dominick, "Film Economics and Film Content: 1964–1983," in *Current Research in Film* (Norwood, N.J.: Ablex, 1987), 144. From 1964–68, sequels and reissues combined accounted for just under five percent of all Hollywood releases. From 1974–78, they comprised 17.5 percent. *Jaws*, for instance, was successfully reissued in 1976, and in 1978 the first of several sequels, *Jaws 2*, was released, returning $49.3 million in rentals and clearly establishing the *Jaws* "franchise."

10 From *The Sound of Music* in 1965 through 1976, only seven pictures (including *Jaws*) had returned $50 million in rentals; in 1977–78 alone, nine films surpassed that mark.

11 J. Hoberman, "Ten Years That Shook the World," *American Film* (June 1985), 42.

12 Hoberman, op cit., and A. D. Murphy, "Twenty Years of Weekly Film Ticket Sales in U.S. Theaters," *Variety*, March 15-21, 1989, 26.

13 "Studio film revenues set to grow by 8.5% in 1995, New Media Markets," May 25, 1995, 9–11. This articles is essentially a synopsis of Goldman Sachs' *Movie Industry Update 1995*, a study done by Richard Simon and Stephen Abraham.

14 *Variety*, Dec 11–17, 1995, 24. In 1995, for example, foreign theatrical revenues for the eight films which grossed at least $100 million in the U.S. was $2.233 billion—well over twice the amount ($1.04 billion) generated in North America. Another interesting fact about the 1995 box office is that the Hollywood studio-distributors saw twice as many films (16) surpass $100 million overseas than reached that figure in North America.

15 John Mickelthwait, "A Survey of the Entertainment Industry," *The Economist*, (December 23, 1989), 5.

16 *Variety*, Jan 8–14, 1996, 8.

17 *Variety*, Jan 8-14, 1996, p. 8. According to Securities Data (*Variety*'s source), there were 306 deals in 1990 for $14.9 billion; 275 deals in 1991 for $13.0 billion; 261 in 1992 for $5.8 billion; 398 in 1993 for $31.5 billion; and 474 in 1994 for $36.1 billion. For profiles of the major media conglomerates in 1995, the year of the second recent major merger wave, see "The Global 50," *Variety*, Aug 28–Sept 3, 1995, 27+.

18 "The Global 50," *Variety*, Aug 28-Sept 1, 1996, 39+. The rankings are based on 1995-96 media revenues, with the top seven companies as follows: Walt Disney Co. ($18.949 billion); Time Warner ($17.696 billion); Bertelsmann AG ($13.7 billion); Viacom Inc. ($11.688 billion); News Corp. ($9.882 billion); Havas ($8.8 billion); and Sony's Entertainment division ($7.696 billion). MCA Inc's media division ranked number 11 (est. $5 billion). Also, Turner Broadcasting System, whose merger with Time Warner was approved since the article appeared, ranked 19th with revenues of $3.437 billion—thus putting the merged Time Warner-Turner ahead of Disney with combined revenues of just over $21 billion.

19 On Disney's annual gross and box-office share, 1990–96, see "EDI Box Office News" (from Entertainment Data Inc.), *Variety*, Dec 9-15, 1996, 22. On Warner Bros., see "EDI Box Office News," *Variety*, Dec 16-22, 1996, 28.

20 On Disney's purchase of Miramax, see *Variety*, May 3 , 1993, 1.

21 *The Economist*, Aug 5, 1995, 5+; *Variety*, Aug 21-27, 1995, 1+; *Variety*, Dec 18-31, 1995, 1+; *Variety*, Jan 8-14, 1996, 1+.

22 *The Economist*, Aug 5, 1995, 56.

23 Time Warner 1986 Annual Report, 6-7.

24 On the Time-Warner merger, see *Variety*, July 26-Aug 1, 1989, 1+; Time Warner Inc.'s 1989 Annual Report to the SEC; *New York Times*, Dec 31, 1990, 21+; *Electronic Media*, Feb 24, 1992, 1+.

25 On the Time Warner-Turner merger, see *Variety*, Sept 25-Oct 1, 1995, 1+; *Variety*, July 26-Aug 1, 1996.

26 *Premiere*, Jan 1996, 76+; *Newsweek*, July 29, 1996, 42+; *Variety*, Sept 23-29, 1996, 1+.

27 *New York Times*, July 5, 1992, f5; *Hollywood Reporter*, Feb 11, 1992, 1+; *Premiere*, Jan 1996, 76.

28 1986 Annual Report of the Walt Disney Company; *Variety*, June 5-11, 1995, 7+; *The Economist*, Aug 5, 1995, 55.

29 Bart in *Variety*, Feb 26-March 3, 1996, 1.

30 *Variety*, Dec 16-22, 1996, 1+; *Variety*, Dec 23, 1996-Jan 5, 1997, 4.

31 For an excellent in-depth account of Disney's mid-1980s management overhaul, see John Taylor, *Storming the Magic Kingdom*, (New York: Knopf, 1987).

32 *Variety*, 18 Oct 93, 1+.

33 *Variety*, 18 Oct 93, 1+.

34 John Seabrook, "Why Is the Force Still With Us?" *The New Yorker*, Jan 6, 1997, 40.

35 *Hollywood Reporter*, Jan 5, 1995, 1+.

36 Corie Brown, "The Years Without Ross," *Premiere*, Jan 96, 78.

37 "'Bat' Blitz Bodes New B.O. Era," *Variety*, June 19-25, 1995, 11+; "Dark Knight Becomes 'Bat' Lite," *Variety*, May 1-7, 1996, 1+.

38 Nancy Haas, "Marvel Superheroes Take Aim at Hollywood," *New York Times*, July 28, 1996, np.

39 *Variety*, May 1-7, 1996, 1+.

40 *Hollywood Reporter*, Feb 6, 1992, 1+; *Variety*, Oct 17-23, 1994, 15+; *Variety*, Nov 21-27, 1994, 18.

41 *Variety*, May 13-19, 1996, 1+. As in almost every phase of the industry, the major studio powers utterly dominate this end of the entertainment market, controlling over 90 percent of the titles. As of May 1996, prior to government approval of the Time Warner-TBS merger, the leading companies and their total holdings were Turner (3,522 titles), Universal (3,101), Sony (2,327), Fox (2,077), Orion (1,986), MGM/UA (1,523),

Warner Bros. (1,102), Paramount (908), and Disney (548).

42 *Newsweek*, July 28, 1996, 42+.

43 *Variety*, Feb 12-18, 1996, 73+; *Variety*, June 24-30, 1996, 7+; *Variety*, Sept 23-29, 1996, np; *Variety*, June 12-25, 1995, 11+; *Variety*, Dec 11-17, 1995, 17+.

44 Kathleen Kernin, "Hi-ho, Hi-ho, A-Marketing We Go...And Go," *Business Week*, June 25, 1990, 54.

45 *Variety*, March 11-17, 1996, 9+.

46 *Variety*, October 14-20, 1996, 1+.

47 *Variety*, October 14-20, 1996, 1+.

48 Figures for 1990 from the Motion Picture Association of America (MPAA) "1990 U.S. Economic Review," 7-8; figures for 1995 from *Variety*, March 11-17, 1996, 9. On ad buys, see *Variety*, March 18-24, 1996, 11.

49 *Variety*, March 18-24, 1996, 11.

50 *Variety*, Sept 30-Oct 6, 1995, np.

51 Internal Disney memorandum of January 11, 1991 from Jeffrey Katzenberg to Michael Eisner, Frank Wells, et al. The memo was leaked to the press and widely publicized; the quotes here are taken from a copy of the original memo, 3, 5, 7, 9.

52 *Variety*, February 4, 1991, 24.

53 Katzenberg memo, 6.

54 *Variety*, Dec 27, 1993, 62.

55 *Variety*, May 6-10, 1996, 10.

56 On the Seagram's sale of Putnam Berkley, see *Variety* Dec 16-22, 1996, 1+. See also *Variety*, Oct 14-20, 1996, 1+.

57 For an excellent in-depth history of the *Star Wars* franchise, see John Seabrook, "Why Is the Force Still With Us?" *The New Yorker*, Jan 6, 1997, 40+.

Mark Crispin Miller

THE PUBLISHING INDUSTRY

Of all the stories that might be told to show what's finally happened to the media, this one tells the saddest story. Gentle reader, here is what the world of letters looks like toward the end of the millennium: it's a small world after all. It might not look small, of course, inside a Borders or a Barnes & Noble, where you can shop for hours, agog at all the "choices"—as you might be at a newsstand, or cruising the TV, or in some multiplex; and the big figures do seem to confirm that dazzled vision of unprecedented cultural bounty: more than $20 billion in U.S. book sales (the most ever!) for 1996, with trade books at an unprecedented $5.7 billion!

And yet that world is very small. Indeed, despite those numbers (which tell half the story), and for all those tons of volumes (most will end up getting pulped), that world is way *too* small. First of all, it's tiny at the top. Aside from W. W. Norton and Houghton Mifflin (the last two major independents), some university presses, and a good number of embattled minors, America's trade publishers today belong to eight gigantic media corporations.[1] In only one of them— Holtzbrinck—does management seem to care (at least for now) what people read. As to the rest, books are—literally—the least of their concerns. For Hearst, Time Warner, Rupert Murdoch's News Corp., the British giant Pearson, the German giant Bertelsmann, Sumner Redstone's Viacom, and S.I. Newhouse's Advance Publications, books count much less than the richer traffic of the newsstands, TV, and the multiplex: industries that were always dominated by a few, whereas book publishing was, once upon a time, a different story.

Too small at the top (and otherwise beset by oligopoly), the trade today has also shrunk in ways that these brief histories may suggest:

LITTLE, BROWN (est. 1837) was one of two great Boston houses that survived the trade's gradual removal to New York. (Houghton Mifflin was the other.) After a staid half-century of local sure things (John Quincy Adams, Francis Parkman) and solid reference works (the *Encyclopedia Britannica*, Bartlett's *Familiar Quotations*), Little, Brown burst into flower, publishing Louisa May Alcott and Emily Dickinson, Balzac and Dumas, Victor Hugo and *All Quiet on the Western Front* (as well as Fannie Farmer's *Cookbook*), to name a few hardy perennials; and then, from 1926 to 1948, under Alfred McIntyre, Little, Brown nurtured authors such as Evelyn Waugh, James Hilton, C. S. Forester, and John P. Marquand—all of whom the beloved McIntyre supported well before the market justified it. Little, Brown was also strong on history (Samuel Eliot Morison, Dumas Malone) and preeminent in books on law.

As part of Time Warner (Time, Inc. bought it in 1968), Little, Brown now mainly sells the product of Time Warner and its mighty peers. In Little, Brown's catalogue for Spring, 1996, we find *Joan Lunden's Healthy Cooking* (ABC/Disney), a bio of La Streisand (Sony), an illustrated "tribute" to Kurt Cobain (MCA), *McCall's Best One-Meal Dishes* (Bertelsmann), *Star Wars: The Death Star* (Fox), *Inside the Titanic* (Fox/Paramount release impending), and Alan Grant's *Batman and Robin*, "based on an original screenplay by Akiva Goldsman," and timed for the impending bat-boom (Warner Bros.) in the multiplexes. There are also several novels that may soon become Time Warner movies—or Sony, or News Corp., or Disney movies: Matthew Hall's *The Art of Breaking Glass* ("breakneck pacing and unrelenting suspense"), David Callahan's *State of the Union* ("breakneck pace and inside-Washington savvy"), Emily Listfield's *The Last Good Night* ("set against the gossip and backbiting of Manhattan's media elite"), George P.

Pelecanis' *King Suckerman* ("a supercharged thriller in the hardboiled tradition of...*Pulp Fiction*").

In these turbid shallows are a few books that are not just marketing: John Fowles' essays, Martin Lee's survey of neo-Nazism. Such exceptions were, however, under budgeted, with next to zip for their promotion, whereas, say, for *Dr. Bob Arnot's Perfect Weight Control for Men and Women* Time Warner shot the works (eleven-city tour, big ads, TV), since Dr. Bob is famous for his health bites on the *CBS Evening News* (Westinghouse) and as a columnist for *Self* (Newhouse). Celebrity counts most at Little, Brown, which—despite the quaint old logo and the offices on Beacon Street—*is* Time Warner. Thus could the house whose credo after 1930 was "Fewer and Better Books" (and which still backlists John H. Wigmore's legal classic, *Evidence*) now be the house that does *I Want To Tell You* "by" O.J. Simpson, for whose warm musings ("I'm a loving guy") Time Warner ultimately paid enough—$1.4 million—to cover his defense.

RANDOM HOUSE (est. 1927) eventually became the largest of the upstart New York houses that awoke the business after World War I. Into what had always been a WASP profession, such ardent Jewish book lovers as Alfred Knopf, Ben Huebsch, and the Boni brothers introduced a spirit of cultural adventure. Thus did the trade take on the glamour of a bold and elegant modernity, as those innovators freely mined the avant-garde, broke ideological taboos, and otherwise took risks—and none took more or better risks than Horace Liveright, Random's accidental father.

As head of Boni and Liveright ("Good Books"), then briefly on his own, that charming and tormented gambler brought American readers every sort of modern classic—and did it lavishly. (His nonchalance soon ruined him.) It was Liveright who first published Faulkner, Hemingway, cummings and Hart Crane, Dorothy Parker, Djuna Barnes and Lewis Mumford; who published Dreiser, Anderson, O'Neill and Pound, *The Waste Land* and *Ten Days That Shook the World*, *Miss Lonelyhearts* and *Gentlemen Prefer Blondes*, *The General Introduction to Psychoanalysis*—Freud's first U.S. title—and three books by Bertrand Russell. (Liveright often braved the censors, twice in court.)

Liveright's cash cow was The Modern Library, which he improvidently sold to Bennett Cerf in 1925. On that rich basis Cerf and Donald Klopfer started Random House, so named because, while fussing over Liveright's baby, they wanted just "to publish a few books on the side at random." Such was the casualness of a venture based on love of books. A far sharper businessman than Liveright (and, unlike him, no leftist), Cerf nonetheless did share with him a lifelong passion for the objects of their trade. Thus Random did *Ulysses* in 1934 (having fought for it in court), and Proust in Scott Moncrieff's translation; soon added over 300 titles to The Modern Library, and created the Modern Library Giants; and ended up as home to an unprecedented range of authors—hard modernists like Auden, Faulkner, and Gertrude Stein; traditional craftsmen like John Cheever and Robert Penn Warren; sure winners like John O'Hara and James Michener; and dubious hits like Ayn Rand and *Masters of Deceit* "by" J. Edgar Hoover.

Random grew so rich that it went public and began to spread; Cerf was eager to get "truly big." In 1960, he and his associates kicked off the Age of Mergers by acquiring Knopf (and Vintage Paperbacks), Beginner Books, the textbook firm I. W. Singer, and then Pantheon in 1961. RCA bought it all in 1965, and in 1980 sold it to S.I. and Donald Newhouse, who by now also own *The New Yorker* and *Vanity Fair*, *Parade*, *Details*, *GQ*, *Gourmet*, and *Vogue* (among other glossies), *and* the nation's fourth-largest newspaper chain, *and* a cable operation—*and* Times Books, Fawcett, Crown, Villard, and Ballantine, all now part(s) of Random House.

As at Little, Brown, the change is total. Here it has been worked, however, not by an apparat of suits but by S. I. Newhouse himself, a hands-on owner like his more infamous junior, Rupert Murdoch. Where Liveright courted T. S. Eliot to get *The Waste Land* (because Pound had recommended it), and where Cerf went to Paris to ask James Joyce for *Ulysses* (because Morris Ernst had pledged to fight the ban in court), S. I. Newhouse made his bones as publisher by getting Donald Trump to do *The Art of the Deal* (because Trump's buss had sent sales of *GQ* through the roof).

Although bullish way back when, Cerf might have had second thoughts if he had known what all the merging would come down to. "Of all the publishing houses in the world, Knopf was the one I had always admired the most." It was Cerf's admiration that encouraged Knopf (and his wife Blanche) to merge with him in 1960—on the "essential condition" that "we shall continue to publish in the future as we have in the past those books in which we believe": i.e., the *best* of literature, whether it might sell or not (and, if not, offset by monsters like *The Prophet*). Recently, Knopf gave us, along with Julian Barnes and Kobo Abe, *¡Delicioso! The Cooking of Regional Spain* and *Eight Weeks to Optimal Healing Power*—both pushed lavishly, while Barnes, Abe, *et al.* went begging. Likewise, Pantheon—"nursed by us to do fine books," as Cerf recalled—was famed for foreign fiction (Gide, Lampedusa, Grass) and distinguished critical analysis (Hobsbawm, Jonathan Schell, the Bollingen series). On one recent list, we had *The American Garden Guide, The Swedish Room* (interior design) and *The Flavors of Bon Appetit, Volume 3*—unlikely books for Pantheon, perhaps, but right for Newhouse, owner of *House and Garden, Architectural Digest* and, of course, *Bon Appetit*.

Thus the new regime is ethically as well as literally deficient. The most scandal-prone of giants, Newhouse's empire often sends its troops across the line, and his generals laugh off all objections. Dick Morris's deal with Random House (and *The New Yorker*) is just the latest instance of such brazenness—which would have horrified S. I.'s predecessor. Cerf deplored the "scandalous" faux-novel about famous people, whom the author slyly limns "in such a way that nobody can mistake who is meant, but also throw[s] in fictional filth, all of which the reader will believe because of the true and recognizable parts." So much for *Primary Colors*. Nor would Cerf have much admired the mercenary lying of Joe Klein (now on staff at *The New Yorker*). Likewise, Cerf was scrupulous in honoring the wishes of Eugene O'Neill, who had sent him *Long Day's Journey into Night* on the condition "that it not be published until twenty-five years after his death." O'Neill's widow wanted it to come out right away, however, and yet "we insisted that Random House could not in conscience publish it." Carlotta took the play to Yale, who got their first best-seller out of it, "but I do not regret that we took the stand we did, because I still think we were right." That code was passé when John Cheever's family went to Random House with his journals—which he, wisely, had not wanted published (and which ran at length in *The New Yorker*).

BANTAM BOOKS (est. 1946) was the second U.S. company to whet the new mass appetite for paperbacks—a momentous trend begun by Pocket Books in 1939. Bantam's aim was doubly democratic. The house was formed by Ian Ballantine, late the head of Penguin's U.S. branch, but thwarted there in his attempt at broad appeal. (He had put pictures on the covers, which Penguin nixed.) For his bid to make good books affordable, Ballantine found backers troubled by a looming threat of giantism: Marshall Field, in 1944, had won control of Simon & Schuster and Pocket Books, and had then gone after Grosset & Dunlap, a hardcover reprint house. Cerf had organized a countermove by several publishers, himself included—because "the thought of one firm…controlled by Marshall Field, having the original publishing unit, the hardbound reprint, and the paperback, too, was frightening." Having rescued Grosset (which it ran peaceably for years), the consortium now helped set Bantam up to compete with Field's colossal Pocket Books.

Ballantine's first list was—and still is—impressive: *Life on the Mississippi*, *The Great Gatsby*, *The Grapes of Wrath*, *What Makes Sammy Run?*, Booth Tarkington's *Seventeen*, Sally Benson's *Meet Me in St. Louis*, and Saint-Exupery's *Wind, Sand and Stars*, as well as several mysteries, Rafael Sabatini's *Scaramouche*, *Rogue Male* by Geoffrey Household—and, for readers young and old, Zane Grey's *Nevada* (although a kid could also read Mark Twain). At 25 cents apiece (even the Steinbeck: 576 pages!), Bantam's offerings were brilliantly competitive with Pocket Books—whose offerings were also good. On *its* first list, Robert De Graff had *Five Great Tragedies* by Shakespeare, *Wuthering Heights, The Way of All Flesh, The Bridge of San Luis Rey, Lost Horizon,* and Dorothy Parker's *Enough Rope,* plus *Topper,* and *The Murder of Roger Ackroyd.* There was also a self-help book called *Wake Up and Live!*—and, for readers young and old, *Bambi* (although a kid could also read Emily Brontë). Thus, facing off, the two firms boomed, and throve until the end.

Today, as part of Bertelsmann (since 1980), Bantam Books does just what you'd expect: *Acupressure for Lovers, Diet 911, Star Wars: The New Rebellion, David Letterman's Second Book of Top Ten Lists,* and *Strong Women Stay Young,* among many others, some hardbound (*The Rocky and Bullwinkle Book,* $50), most in paper (*The Aerobics Program for Total Well-Being,* $16.95).[2] Surely old and young alike can read the *Star Wars* books, or, say, Mark Fabi's *Wyrm* ("a rocketing millennial thriller")—but Bantam also has a cool new series out for (male) preteens: "Barf-o-Rama" offers them *The Great Puke-Off, The Legend of Bigfart,* and *Dog Doo Afternoon,* among other titles. These tales of "fettuccine al farto," "buttwurst," and "scab pie" are certainly a world apart from Bantam's *Flavors of the Riviera*: a range that shows how broad the vision is at Bertelsmann. (Meanwhile, Pocket Books is publisher of *Beavis and Butthead: This Book Sucks.*)

Critiques of our mass culture are, of course, not much liked by those who've made a lot of money trashing it. This is especially true of publishing, which—unlike the movies, TV, radio, the press—was not, until some years ago, a profit-centered venture but a true labor of love. That odd history makes the vandals of the trade a bit defensive. "I've always thought it profoundly wrong to say that it used to be better in the old days," says Viacom's Michael Korda, who remembers Cerf, Klopfer, and the Knopfs as "stingy"—and just as grasping as any oligopolist today. Publishing, superagent Morton Janklow once remarked, "is, after all, a business that people went into for profit, even in former times." Before the trust absorbed it, the trade was frozen with "elitism," according to Dick Snyder, tough ex-CEO of Simon & Schuster.

Scorned at the top, critiques like this one also tend to be more generally offensive—because they threaten the great myth that we today have *more* and infinitely *better* "choices" than our poor parents did with their three channels and two colas. Surely, anyone who knocks the product out there now is a nostalgic crank, pining for a "golden age" that never was, etc. Surely anyone who takes a hard look back at what folks really used to read will see that most of it was always lousy—just like now. "'Twas ever thus: anyone who imagines that a hundred years ago Americans were rushing out to buy the new Henry James is kidding himself," writes Anthony Lane in *The New Yorker*.

Of course, the common run of literature has always been just that. Revisit any seeming "golden age" and read it *all*, and what you'll find is mostly dreck. Here, it was mostly dreck when Liveright was in flower, as in England, even back when Dickens, Thackeray, Trollope and George Eliot were also writing, it was mostly dreck; and, prior to that, throughout the first great "golden age" of English fiction—Fielding, Richardson, Tobias Smollett, Laurence Sterne—dreck ruled. "In the miscellanies of the eighteenth century," Professor Robert Mayo tells us, "there is only feeble evidence for a prelapsarian age in literary culture." And even earlier, in the most golden age of all, Shakespeare was the one and only, towering high above his few noteworthy peers—and in a universe apart from that obscure majority whose hack work kept the theatres going.

So there's been no golden age—and yet books have gotten worse: worse in every way. Although what's bad is always with us, first of all, *this* stuff takes the cake. Peruse the offerings of Harper & Row and William Collins, and try to find among them any volume of nonfiction as half-baked, ill-informed, and crudely written as Newt Gingrich's *To Renew America*, or as prolix, muddled and me-me-me-me as Nancy Friday's *The Power of Beauty*—to name two from HarperCollins. Try to find, in all the major houses' prior lists, any memoir as empty and self-serving as *I Want To Tell You*, or *My Story* "by Sarah, Duchess of York" (Viacom). And try to find, on any lists, a book, for children, about boogers, farts, or puking.

Low intellectually—and morally, as William Bennett might care to observe (although his publisher is also Butthead's)—books have worsened, too, in their material craftsmanship. The trade now deals in shoddy goods because of widespread editorial neglect. Where the independent houses prized the subtle labor of their editors, the giants want their people not to be agonizing over prose but signing big names over lunch. Thus countless books today are tediously flawed—rambling, incoherent, repetitious, and obese—because they've each been vetted only by the author's friends and family.

Such inattention caused the worst of 1995's literary scandals: the decision by St. Martin's to do—then not do—David Irving's rapt biography of Josef Goebbels. Although deeply partial (at times it seems that Dr. Goebbels himself wrote it), the book does contain enough new information to have justified an effort to de-Nazify it. An editor appropriately thorough would have cut the starker bits of anti-Semitism, made Irving drop the howlers based exclusively on Nazi sources, and urged him to play down his weakness for the Führer. The book would have been much shorter, saner and more edifying than the big sick mess that St. Martin's ended up so ignominiously killing because no one there had read it.

Such delinquency is now epidemic, as book reviews suggest—for the harsh ones often turn on defects that ought to have been caught by an editor. Thus, within the few recent months, *The New York Times Book Review* scored the bloatedness (550 pages) of HarperCollins' *An Easy Burden* by Andrew Young, who "accords the same detail to devouring slabs of ribs and bowls of gumbo as he does to the tear-gassing of black marchers in Selma in 1965"; deplored the excess (557 pages) in Knopf's *Clint Eastwood* by Richard Schickel (who "can't restrain himself from bland talk and gassy moralizing"); observed the "critical structural flaw" that ruins Mark Singer's book about Brett Kimberlin (from Knopf, after a piece in *The New Yorker*); complained that Michael J. Mandel's *The High-Risk Society* (Random House) is "long on generality and annoying repetition," and that Marc Parent's *Turning Stones* (Harcourt) "often clunks with images like 'the hairs on the back of my neck slowly rotating in their follicles.'" Nor do the books thus hit come only from the giants—Oxford did Norman Davies' massive *Europe*, with its "inaccuracies [on] every other page," and Henry Holt did *No Hands: The Rise and Fall of the Schwinn Bicycle Company*—a book yet to be written: "Within this march of facts lurks an absorbing case study, at perhaps half the length."

Unread by its editor, the text today is also left untouched by proofreaders: not out of indolence, but because they've all been fired. Such low-paid perfectionists were the first to go when publishing went global. They were replaced with even lower-paid freelancers—and the giants often skimp further by eliminating galleys, so that manuscripts go straight to page proofs. Thus, we now see typos everywhere. They litter Eric Hobsbawm's *The Age of Extremes*, a noble holdover from Pantheon ("industralization," "Westen countries"), as they do Richard Gid Powers' *Not Without Honor: A History of American Anticommunism*, a dog from the Free Press ("blacks members," "propandistic," "they were able from give the country")—and Tom Dardis' *Firebrand*, a fine biography of Horace Liveright, published not too carefully by Random House ("distain," Ivor "Montague," "Ogonquit"). And to see how Random prizes Liveright's legacy, check out the latest Modern Library edition (1993) of *The Wings of the Dove*, in which, e.g., "Densher hoped for visit," "he" appears as "she," and "Mrs. Stringham mainly failed of ease mainly failed of ease in respect to her own consistency." (Elsewhere she is "Mrs. Strigham.")

And as books were better than they are today, so were their publishers *not* profit-driven. Yes, they wanted to make money; but they could have made much more in other fields—if only they were not in love with books. "In my soul was an insatiable longing to be back among books, the discovery of them, the making of them, and the selling and distribution of them," George Doran wrote of a youthful stint in realty. Incomprehensible today, that passion drove the publishers of yore. "A good book," wrote Dutton's Elliott Macrae, "means to each of us hours of absorbed interest, of sheer delight and appreciation, an alertness, a quickening of mind and heart such as can never be achieved in any other fashion." With that odd joy no profiteering can compete. "Every true book lover reads," Charles Scribner, Jr., said not long ago, "with a kind of pleasure that is akin to eating."

Certainly, they did their share of the eternal dreck; but for them it was a necessary evil—and that, finally, is the crucial difference between then and now. As book lovers *and* businessmen, they did the high-yield trash in order to be able to afford the gems they loved (although the gems might also sell). "A publisher of books," Doran advised, must "be a mixed farmer, sow first in this field and then in that, and rotate his crops, if he is successfully to distribute his product." Not all of them were so resigned. "The books that Alfred is most ashamed of are the ones that have made him the most money!" Cerf said of Knopf, who hated having published Harold Robbins and Kahlil Gibran. Whether cool about it or "ashamed" of it, however, those publishers would now and then do crap—to use Doran's conceit—so as to help some finer things to grow; whereas today crap is not a means but (as it were) the end.

That shift was not dictated by today's octopoly, but started in the sixties, and came from several factors. The ruinous overvaluation of best-sellers—"the blockbuster complex," as Thomas Whiteside called it[3]—was, first of all, an economic consequence of the great boom in subsidiary rights: book club and, especially, paperback rights. As the paperback houses were, throughout the go-go years, paying hardcover publishers ever higher prices to reprint the hottest titles, the value of subsidiary rights exploded—until the publishers were making more on those once-secondary deals than on their own hardcover sales. Soon dependent on such income (in 1979, Crown sold Bantam the reprint rights to *Princess Daisy* for over $3 million), the publishers were less interested in finding "the best books" than in cultivating this or that potential monster. (Now that the giants also do the paperbacks, such competition has waned.)

Meanwhile, the sway of hype had been enlarged a millionfold by TV, in whose national sales arena modest readerships seemed ever less worthwhile. It started early: Prentice-Hall did Art Linkletter's *Kids Say the Darndest Things* in 1957, and the book—flogged weekly by the author on his show—was a best-seller for over a year; and Simon & Schuster got two big winners out of Alexander King, a witty regular on Jack Paar's *Tonight Show*. Soon TV was not a golden opportunity (as Cerf, for one, believed) but a grim necessity, with the trade obliged to get its larger authors byting on as many shows as possible—*Today*, *Tomorrow*, Johnny, Merv, and Donahue. Today, what with TV's even tighter grip, the giants are even deeper into it, staying close to shows like *60 Minutes*, *20/20* and—above all—*Oprah* (whose "Book Club" can increase sales by as much as 3,000 percent). The books thus plugged are few—and none of them will blow your mind, since TV likes friendly monosyllables and authors with great hair, thereby forcing the survival of the cutest.

The bias toward lite books has been steepened also by the heavy concentration at the sales end of the business: a field long shadowed by bookstore chains, but whose seizure by a few has lately reached the crisis point. By 1980, the two leading chains—B. Dalton and Waldenbooks—had reduced the independents' market share to less than 40 percent. Today, that scrap looks ample, now that countless independents have been broken by those two hip predators, Borders (which now owns Waldenbooks) and Barnes & Noble. Whereas the prior chains once stayed mainly in suburbia, the Big Two take over city blocks, often near each other—going head to head, to wipe each other out.

While it offers some ephemeral benefit to local shoppers—kids' programs, folk music, good espresso—that corporate feud is, in the long run, only further narrowing the culture. The gross demand of those commercial fortresses requires the giants to provide them with the dumbest titles in fantastic quantities: enough to fill each fortress with proud towers of, say, *Airframe*—an in-store promotional boost for which the giants pay the superstores (who also sell window placement). The independent stores get no such subsidy; and that collusion also hurts the smaller houses, who lack the cash to have their books heaped up so awesomely.[4]

Then there's the practice of returns. The superstores have generally ordered tons more books than they could ever sell—and then paid for those they've sold by sending back the ones they haven't. This titanic ripoff has distorted the whole trade. While the Big Two do, in fact, stock more small-press titles than the independent bookstores can, they also "pay" the smaller houses with returns; and those houses can't afford it, while the giants—with their bad dailies, cable TV, talk-radio, etc.—have sufficient capital to take the hit. But the giants too are losing; and so they spend still more to push their crudest items, and that much less (if anything) to find the smaller market for their mid-list titles. (Those items sit not only in the superstores but in air-ports, supermarkets, Wal-Marts—venues that now sell more books than bookstores do.)[5]

While the Big Two have gotten lots of press, the trade is lessened also by yet another less visible duopoly. Book distribution now belongs to just two national companies: Ingram and Baker & Taylor. The two, in fact, have gone beyond mere distribution to the active marketing of books to Barnes & Noble and Borders, a service only the giants can afford. The distributors can also hurt the little guy in other ways, their size enabling them to pay their bills when they feel like it—a casual-ness inimical to modest publishers. Last fall, having tried for months to collect $300,000 that Ingram owed him, Lyle Stuart, owner of Barricade Books, told them he was through with them—and so they stopped the little check they'd sent him ($30,000), and dropped Blue Moon Books, an imprint listed in his catalogue. "Small publishers are not being paid, or are not being paid enough to keep them in business," Stuart said. "Ingram is so huge, they feel you can't do business without them. But we can't stay in business if we keep dealing with them."

Finally, the giants' drift toward dreck has been accelerated also by the mad increase, since the sixties, in the sums they pay up front to lure the "hot." Now that all the imprints are unstable, with editors forever leaving, writers go from house to house not searching for a home but looking for the sweetest deal. As elsewhere in the culture of TV, such epidemic self-promotion has made stars out of certain agents, who have lately jacked advances up to drug-lord levels: $2.5 million for Dick Morris (Newhouse), more than $5 million for General Schwarzkopf (Bertelsmann), $6.5 million for General Powell (Newhouse), $3.5 million for Paula Barbieri (Time Warner), $6 million for Whoopi Goldberg (Hearst), etc. Up top, it's all a gas. "This is a business where everybody breaks out the champagne when they spend millions of dollars on a book," one HarperCollins veteran sighed in 1990. Dazzled by big names and heady numbers—as in Hollywood—the giants' editors seem strangely careless as to whether this or that big book will ever make the money back. Nor do they mind the gross inequity of those advances—because of which so many other authors just scrape by, or simply don't get published.

Although the giants did not create this system, they are themselves the biggest problem with it, for it is they—and not the TV-addled masses, or the bursting superstores or greedy agents—who have done the most to wreck the trade. "It's hard to find an industry that has been picked cleaner by the conglomerates than book publishing," *Forbes* observed in 1981. That industry has now been picked to death by its own parents, who would, it seems, do *anything* to books, and to the culture, for the sake of profits.

From their book units, first of all, they now want profits way too high for publishing, which never yielded high returns: "For the truth is," as British bookman Michael Joseph wrote in 1949, "that no publisher worth his salt cares about his balance sheets provided that he can live." This was no bull. For decades, notes André Schiffrin, the trade throve on an after-taxes profit rate of roughly 4 percent, most of it reinvested. Likewise, today's last few great French houses prosper modestly: Gallimard makes just over 3 percent; Le Seuil just over 1 percent. By contrast, the giants expect their houses to show profits of from 12 to 15 percent—comparable to what they make off movies, dailies, and TV—but finally, percentages quite impossible for publishing.

And even if they made it, it would never be enough: "If someone does make 15 percent," writes Schiffrin, "the others are expected to do the same, and the unfortunate front runner is then expected to make 16 percent." That compulsion is irrational, despite the frequent numbers and the canny talk of "competition": S. I. Newhouse and his brother Donald, for example, share the nation's largest private fortune (now over $10 billion)—and yet their houses are on permanent alert, as if their peerless empire were on the verge of going under. Such paranoia has undone the industry, degrading not just books but the profession that creates them.

Before the giants came, it was a great way to make a modest living. "A job with any publishing house was a plum," recalled Lillian Hellman, "but a job with Horace Liveright was a bag of plums." Cerf, too, ran a friendly house where the editors did what they liked—but now live in fear, their napes chilled always by the shadow of the axe. Under Newhouse, there was Schiffrin, Robert Bernstein, Elisabeth Sifton, Peter Osnos. The list of those beheaded suddenly at Random House tells us that the world of books is now as nasty as the world of advertising. The pressure is incessant—and direct. "Si is really yanking Alberto's chain," one insider said last fall of Random's CEO Alberto Vitale, to explain the firing of Osnos, publisher of Times Books—which thenceforth "would be doing less nonfiction" and more of what makes money" according to Harold Evans, Random House's president (i.e., crossword puzzles and books on health). The Newhouse push has not just dumbed books down, but wiped them out: Schiffrin recalls Vitale's order that any title selling fewer than two thousand copies yearly must be pulped.

No book lover would do that, but there are few such rare birds at the top. On the contrary, with the houses now absorbed into the media trust, its top dogs tend to relegate the trade to others like themselves— not readers, nor even lucid speakers of the language. This is true not only of the Hollywood imprints, like Disney's Hyperion and Viacom's MTV Books. In 1996, Avon announced a three-year, thirty-title deal with Brandon Tartikoff, one-time programming whiz at NBC ("It's time for a daffy female," he once urged a producer) and more recently a big editor at Warner Books, where he also scouted titles for Disney's Miramax. Inclined, pre-Hearst, to push neglected U.S. writers (the house did Henry Roth's *Call It Sleep* in 1964), through Tartikoff Books Avon will show a different bias: "I think when you hear a star is interested in a film project, it could lend itself to a book property," Tartikoff told *Publishers Weekly*. "Some things can be baked into the literary work."

Likewise, Michael Lynton, CEO and chairman of the Penguin Group for Pearson, was formerly a suit at Disney, where he ran Hollywood Pictures—helping them produce, among other gems, Demi Moore's *The Scarlet Letter*, with its happy ending. Lynton quickly made a place ("Senior Editor, West Coast") for Angela Janklow Harrington, daughter of superagent Mort Janklow, wife of Gerry Harrington (talent manager at Brillstein-Grey) and editor of *Mouth-2-Mouth*, an L.A.-based teenzine that lasted months. "I'll be using my connections to sign up celebrities and brainstorming concepts," she told the *New York Observer*. "I'll go after some traditional celebrity biographies, but because I know aspects of certain people that are inimitably theirs, it will be even more along the lines of the next *Sein Language*, or finding the next Deepak Chopra." Whatever that means, Ms. Harrington will work hard for the money, often jetting in from Hollywood for face-time with her peers at Penguin U.S.A. ("I like to have a visual with the people I'm working with," she explains.)

Just as diligent is HarperCollins' CEO Anthea Disney (no relation to Walt), whose previous work for Rupert Murdoch included running *TV Guide*—goosing up its numbers with a *People*-style "who's hot" section called "Insider" and, on every other cover, hunks flexing or babes pouting. (Like Tina Brown at *The New Yorker*, Disney also uses the big weekly to hype its owner's other properties.) Under Murdoch, such experience is all you need to run a house; Disney had none in publishing when Murdoch (who has none) appointed her. But she now knows it all, as she assured her authors in a recent letter: "As CEO of Harper for the past ten months, I've had a uniquely hands-on opportunity to observe the day-to-day publishing activities of the company." Her next line says much about the trade today: "I have worked directly with all aspects of the publishing process: editorial, marketing, design, etc.; an eye-opening experience with an extraordinary learning curve."

The invasion of the media people has helped turn books into TV. There are, of course, all those fast-moving items written "by" such telestars as Leno, Oprah, Ellen, and Tim Allen—and the newest faces, too, will soon be mugging at us from a million dust jackets: ABC's Drew Carey, & MTV's Jenny McCarthy. Then there are the novels that, if they don't somehow end up *as* TV, are *like* TV, with its crass glamour, loud simplicity, and "breakneck pace"—the very titles (*Absolute Power, Total Control, Primary Colors, Intensities*) reflecting on the media trust's own global sway and irresistible f/x.

And in their form too, books have been made televisual by those who cut their teeth in TV or at *TV Guide*. Consider Anthea Disney's claim that "editorial" is just another "aspect of the publishing process," equal to design and marketing, which are, in fact, what matter *most* to those types trained to make you grab a tabloid or sit through a sitcom. Thus, while the text may be a shambles, the cover took some time since, in this universe, the packaging counts most. "We're trying to communicate a feeling or mood that will attract impulse buyers," remarks a Berkley editor.

The same desire to please is also giving us nonfiction stripped of its least viewer-friendly features. Certainly the footnote is in trouble, having been declared a no-no even at the academic presses, which now, perforce, are also crowding into Borders. "Our marketing department tells us that footnotes scare off people," says an editor at Harvard—and so, perhaps, it should be unsurprising that there are no notes in, say, John Keegan's *Fields of Battle* (Knopf), Thomas Hines' *The Total Package* (Little, Brown), Richard Meryman's biography of Andrew Wyeth (HarperCollins), or Edvard Radzinsky's *Stalin* (Doubleday). On the other hand, it is surprising that so many nonfiction books now lack an *index*, as if that elementary guide might also "scare off" would-be readers stunned by channel surfing. Thus Walter Cronkite's and David Brinkley's slight memoirs (Knopf) are both index-free, as are David Foster Wallace's essays (Little, Brown) and Jane Kramer's book on modern Germany, *The Politics of Memory* (Random House).

As the media people have worsened books to grow the bottom line (to use the famed locution of a certain Random author), so have the owners, albeit in a more titanic way. With publishing the least of their concerns, the giants have often used it to improve their business somewhere else, or overall—a strategy of acquisition that has, inevitably, given us some books that stink (and that didn't sell).

The best-known of such operators is, of course, Rupert Murdoch, who has used his houses just as he has used, say, the *New York Post* and London *Times*: to soft-soap any politician he might need. Thus his authors include Newt Gingrich, Margaret Thatcher—and Deng Maomao, Deng Xiaoping's daughter, who Murdoch hoped might help him get her government to let him broadcast Sky TV in China. To that end, he had BasicBooks put out the English version of her *Deng Xiaoping: My Father*, a thick dose of the sort of propaganda that comes squawking through loud speakers in Beijing. ("His smile," she writes of the old killer, "transcends the range of time and space and is eternal.") The book—like Newt's—died quickly but, of course, that was beside the point.

Less notorious than Murdoch, but no less canny, is his quieter compeer, S. I. Newhouse—who is not just President Clinton's publisher (and Bill Bradley's, and Jimmy Carter's), but who also bankrolled Colin Powell's bid for the White House in 1995. It was his tour to promote *My American Journey*—and the $6+ million advance—that enabled General Powell to toss his stars into the ring; nor were his chances hurt by the puff pieces in *Parade*, *Vanity Fair*, and *The New Yorker*. "The candidate from Random House," he was called by Maureen Dowd—one of the few who marked the fact that publishing has now become the sport of kingmakers.

Indeed, S. I.'s story is unknown to most. With his downmarket appeal and hard-right influence (the *Post*, *The Weekly Standard*; Oliver North's *Under Fire*, etc.), the ex-Australian is an easy target for the educated (just like Nixon, with whom he has a lot in common). Meanwhile, for all *his* power—that is, because of it—S.I. Newhouse is almost never mentioned, much less criticized. As Ronald

Reagan was our teflon president, S. I. Newhouse is our great stealth mogul; and his invisibility brings us to the most dangerous consequence of the decline of publishing.

"Book publication," Curtice Hitchcock wrote in 1937, "is the freest form of expression we have, and the one in which the time-honored principle of freedom of speech is observed better than anywhere else." It was precisely because of its small scale that that culture industry was thus unique: "The large circulation magazine, the newspaper, the motion picture, or the radio program, since they are intended for a mass audience, must perforce avoid taboos held sacred by any substantial portion of that audience, or they fail. A book can, and to a considerable extent does, find its own level of taste, appreciation, and intelligence." In that quiet, gradual way, the book might make you think, might help you see. "If the book is important, however unpalatable it may be to large groups of people, the author can feel with some measure of truth that despite a small sale his ideas have been started in circulation and may seep (as ideas have a way of doing) beyond the range of the actual cash customers."

A long shot at the best of times, such dissemination is unlikelier than ever, now that publishing is part of TV. The slow course of an idea or vision through some dispersed subculture of thoughtful readers (as opposed to the endless wildfire on the Internet) is hardly possible when those who own the trade want only big returns right now. Thus have the giants shrunk the culture in part automatically, by imposing that objective "market censorship" whereby (say) Pantheon went from doing Hans Magnus Enzensberger, Marguerite Duras, and Martin Walker to doing *Water Gardening* and *Decorating Magic.*

However, the giants have shrunk the culture not just by flooding it with trivia, but also by discouraging, or dumping, those books that offer revelations irksome to the giants themselves, and/or some other super-power(s). The distention of the trade, in other words, has limited our freedom of expression not just because the masses are too pious (a touchiness less influential now than sixty years ago), but because the owners—and their friends—have much to hide.

This fact may help explain the rightward drift of publishing since 1980. Where Knopf *et al.* were left-of-center (although catholic in their literary tastes), and often fought for free expression, the giants are not so much "conservative" as tellingly hospitable to those who hate that freedom: Representative Gingrich, full-time campaigner against "liberal thinking"; Lady Thatcher, dedicated to making socialism "inconceivable"; Judge Bork, with his livid "case for censorship" to thwart "the forces of decadence"; Deng Maomao, apostle of her dad's heroic work "disseminating the Party's ideology and cultural knowledge"; Colonel North, who sees the press as locked in Manichaean opposition to the Bible; and General Powell, talented upholder of the U.S. military's right to keep the people in the dark, as his service—and his book—make clear.

By promoting such repressive types the culture trust betrays its own censorious impulse. True, the giants churn out all that stuff the would-be commissars deplore: "Look at the sick signals we are now sending through the entertainment industry and popular culture," cries Newt, and Bork laments that "American popular culture is in a free fall, with the bottom not yet in sight." There seems to be some tension there—and yet with such vague diatribe the giants can and do live easily: Murdoch had no trouble publishing those two, even as he publishes Boy George. What he and his peers do not want, and what they never will allow, is a critique that gets specific, and that clearly lays the blame where it belongs—not on "ourselves," or on "the liberal view of human nature" (to quote two Borkisms), but on the oligopoly that has long since sold the culture out.

The giants will, it seems, do anything to jolt us, stroke us, goose us, make us hurl; and yet they'd never want to shake us up *too* much, or we might start putting two and two together. Thus their books are ever more "provocative," but only superficially—titillating, tantalizing, nauseating. ("He was the kind of man who was too busy to flush the toilet," begins Mona Simpson's *A Regular Guy*, from Knopf.) Meanwhile, today's writers are as free to tell hard truths about the ruling powers as they would be under Colonel North—or as they are in China.

Sharp books on the giants quickly end up on the same unspoken *index librorum prohibitorum* that also lists the trustiest books on U.S. foreign policy–books known only to some academics and other such selective cranks, so effective is that index. The books thereon have been dispatched in various ways. In 1973, Warner Communications actually shut down an imprint rather than do *The Political Economy of Human Rights* by Noam Chomsky and Edward Herman (who went to South End Press). More recently, some first-rate studies of the CIA were killed adroitly. Christopher Simpson's classic *Blowback*, on the agency's heavy use of ex-fascists during the Cold War, was panned in the *New York Times Book Review* by Serge Schmemann–son of an ecclesiastical ally of war-time mass murderer Valerian Trifa–while Herbert Mitgang's glowing notice for the daily *Times* was spiked abruptly, no explanation given. (*Blowback* is out of print.) Simpson's next, *The Splendid Blond Beast*, got no big reviews except a tepid one in the *Washington Post*–by Alan Ryan, whose work Simpson had attacked, although Ryan did not mention that. Then most of the first print run was lost by Grove, and finally found–too late–in an Appalachian warehouse. (Common Courage does it now.)

On Burton Hersh's *The Old Boys*, a subtle history of the CIA and Wall Street, the *Times Book Review* ran a muddled hatchet-job that Hersh refuted in a letter to the editors (who, oddly, also ran a snide reply from the reviewer). CIA contacts told Hersh that some "important figures" in the agency had put out a call for errors they could use against him; Scribner felt the heat, cut back Hersh's tour and ran no ads. "They didn't want to live with the flak it would have engendered if it sold," he says. (Steerforth Press now does it.) Lately we have Frank Kofsky's superb *Harry S. Truman and the War Scare of 1948* from St. Martin's, reviewed (by Chomsky) in *In These Times* and nowhere else; and Gerard Colby's and Charlotte Dennett's astonishing *Thy Will Be Done*–an epic study of how Nelson Rockefeller used U.S. evangelicals to help "pacify" the Amazon–published, then dropped like a hot potato, by HarperCollins, after few reviews. With books so solid and eye-opening, such eerie quiet is no accident, as John Loftus learned from someone at the CIA. As an ex-assistant to the Attorney General (in the Nazi War Crimes unit), Loftus must let Langley vet his work, and did so with *The Secret War Against the Jews* (St. Martin's), his and Mark Aarons' dark history of the CIA's relations with big oil. The manuscript would be okayed, he heard—"but you'll never get a review in America." If you haven't heard about the book (which made headlines abroad), that may be why.

This being the national entertainment state, however, books are also killed right in New York, or Hollywood, without a word from Langley. Full of creepy news about its subject (FBI fink, antisemite), Marc Eliot's *Walt Disney: Hollywood's Dark Prince* was aborted suddenly by Bantam in 1991, because, his editor said, it was "not of publishable quality"—although he'd only sent some notes. Eliot then learned of Bantam's plan to do the "Disney Library" for sale in supermarkets—a deal worth far more than his book would have been. (It later came from Birch Lane Press, to strong reviews, then disappeared.) In 1993, Robert Sam Anson's book on the Disney studios was—after four years of research—stopped dead by Simon & Schuster, evidently because Marvin Davis, head of Paramount (S&S's then-owner) and a player in Disney's history, didn't want the press. (That book never did get written.) And Christopher Byron's *Skin Tight: The Bizarre Story of Guess v. Jordache*, although slated for a big print run and loud release, crashed badly when they learned at S&S that a crucial figure in the book was now the wife of Stanley Jaffe, president of Paramount. Byron tried to cut out every mention, but he couldn't cut them all, so they slashed the print run, canned his tour and ran no ads. (That book is gone.)

While killing books distasteful to its bosses (or their wives), the media trust can also flood the world with its own sunny counter-story. Starting in December, 1979, all copies of *Katherine the Great*, Deborah Davis' life of Katherine Graham, were pulped by Harcourt Brace Jovanovich, despite the house's late enthusiasm for the work (which it was going to name for an American Book Award). HBJ had been spooked (so to speak) by a very threatening letter from Ben Bradlee, attacking Davis' claims that Graham had CIA connections. (The bio came out later, and invisibly, from National Books.) Now Graham's own 625-page *Personal History* has been promoted with much help from her machine: cover story in the *Post*'s Sunday mag, a rave in that day's "Book World," then excerpts in the *Post*'s Style section and in *Newsweek*, etc. Detailed as it is, this *History* never mentions Davis—or the background of the *Post*'s best-known reporter: "Woodward had come to us fresh from the navy," Graham writes tersely, thus erasing Bob's pre-*Post* years in military intelligence, and his duties, in 1969-70, as the Joint Chiefs' liaison with the NSC's Al Haig, whom he regularly briefed in Nixon's White House basement (facts documented in some books from Birch Lane and St. Martin's).[6]

The bigger the mogul, the deader any book that might offend him—a truth reconfirmed by the Orwellian experience ("You do not exist") of Thomas Maier, *Newsday* reporter and the author of a recent book on publishing's Big Tuna. Of S.I.'s rise to dominance *Newhouse* tells the whole absorbing story: the newspaper monopolies built up in city after city; the commercialist aesthetic of the magazines, whose articles are *meant* to look like ads; one of the biggest tax-evasion trials in U.S. history—a contest fumbled by the IRS; Newhouse's lifelong friendship with Roy Cohn, through whom the family helped Joe McCarthy, Jackie Presser, and the Chicago mob; and all those brusque beheadings at Random, Conde Nast and *The New Yorker*. Thorough and low-key (and laying off the private life), *Newhouse* is a sobering "parable on American media power"—but what befell it is, on that subject, almost as edifying as the book itself.

At the start, no-one would touch it—not even in London, where the Bloomsbury Press responded typically: "'We love it, but we're sorry, we do business with S.I. Newhouse,'" Maier recalls.[7] St. Martin's finally took the book—and had a hard time selling it: *Vanity Fair* refused an ad, and Liz Smith's bit was oddly missing from her column in that day's Newhouse newspapers. The book was not reviewed or even mentioned in *New York*; and, in the city, Maier also found *himself* blacklisted. Although Dr. Spock had granted him permission—and full access—for the first-ever biography, Maier had "become persona non grata with about 40 percent of the book publishing world." When Crown discovered who he was, they quickly cancelled his appointment to discuss the project.

And so *Newhouse* sank (although it won Tau Kappa Alpha's prestigious Frank Luther Mott Research Award for "best media book" of 1994). The paperback came out in 1996—from Johnson Books in Boulder, Colorado.

And so Borders' offering is not as comprehensive as it looks. For all the books that do shine there, important others can't. And among the missing in the superstores are also many titles wiped out not by corporate whim but by a stroke of Federal stupidity. In 1979, the Supreme Court upheld the IRS by ruling that tool companies could not write off the costs of warehouse inventory. Soon the IRS applied the rule to publishers, as if books were drill-bits—and so the giants' back-lists have been stripped of every title that is not forever "hot": *The Sexual Enlightenment of Children, The Stepford Wives* and *Good As Gold*, Malraux's *Anti-Memoirs*, Steven Marcus' *The Other Victorians*, Garry Wills' *Reagan's America*, Brooke Hayward's *Haywire*, Andy Warhol's *A* and countless other worthy books are out of print— as is Thomas Whiteside's *The Blockbuster Complex* (and every other book used for this essay).

Thus is a title's shelf-life now its *whole* life—and the span grows ever less. While we lack hard numbers on it, those who know say that most new books have about as long to live as most TV shows. But even such big items as Lou Cannon's *President Reagan: The Role of a Lifetime* (S&S: 1991) can't stay in print; and so the giants' mid-list books, deprived from birth, now have the life expectancy of houseflies. Such easy disappearance speeds the culture's rightward thrust, as critical works vanish, revisionism takes their place and right-wing houses—private sustained—keep ancient screeds in print. While Regnery does Jonathan Aitken's loving life of Nixon (and Whittaker Chambers' *Witness,* and his correspondence with Bill Buckley), gone are Bruce Oudes' *From: The President,* William Shawcross' *Sideshow,*

Jonathan Schell's *Observing the Nixon Years*, Tad Szulc's *The Illusion of Peace* and Seymour Hersh's *The Price of Power*—as are Dan Moldea's *Dark Victory*, Mark Hertsgaard's *On Bended Knee*, Harrison Salisbury's *Without Fear or Favor*, nearly all George Seldes' writings and a whole library of other savvy works on politics and media.

And what of the alternative—the independents and the university presses? Many independents are worrying that they may not make it through the year, as libraries cut back on orders and returns keep pouring in. Meanwhile, the academic houses are now pressed by cost-conscious university administrators to make it on their own, without institutional subsidies. Thus those houses too are giving in to market pressure, dumping recondite monographs in favor of trendier academic fare or, better yet, whatever sells at Borders—which, presumably, means few footnotes. Those publishers are so hard pressed there's talk in the academy of changing tenure rules, because it's next to impossible to get an arcane study published—a dark development indeed.

Defenders of the system like to charge its critics with elitism. That pseudo-populist stance is quite belied by the history of publishing, which at its best had always sought mass readership. "He was a genius at devising ways to put books into the hands of the unbookish," Edna Ferber said of Nelson Doubleday. "A publisher who can do that is as important—or nearly—as Gutenberg." If today's giants are so good at selling to the people, why is the trade in trouble? Like the culture trust's big movies and CDs, its books are mostly duds: Last summer was the worst season in five years, with returns as high as, or exceeding, 40 percent of gross sales.

Inside a Barnes & Noble or Borders, such failure is not obvious—nor is the actual sameness underlying all that seeming multiplicity. Look closer, and you'll see how many of those new books from Hyperion are merely ads for Disney—including Oprah's aptly titled *Make the Connection* (she and Disney have a multi-picture deal).

Find *The New Yorker* on the magazine rack, and chances are that the issue's fiction, or nonfiction, came from one of S. I. Newhouse's houses. (Last year more than half the magazine's twenty-six excerpts came from Random titles.) Look too at Random's books on *other* giants, and note how uncritical they are—Kay Graham's memoir (Knopf) and Steven Cuozzo's *It's Alive* (Times Books), a paean to Rupert Murdoch.

Then think ahead, imagining the day when either Barnes & Noble or Borders wins their war—and try to picture what that seeming multiplicity will look like. When there's just one chain left, its superstores will not be ordering those offbeat books from the remaining small houses, which will then fold. For those who like to read, the prospect is a frightening one, but not as frightening as the fact that people won't know what they're missing. Before that happens, we should ask some serious questions about culture and democracy—and antitrust—before there's nothing left to help us answer them.

1   Of educational publishers, there now are only three huge parents, Viacom, McGraw-Hill and Harcourt General.

2   Having been absorbed into the media trust, the paperback giants started hardcover divisions in the Eighties.

3   *The Blockbuster Complex* (Wesleyan University Press, 1981) is out of print. See also Lewis Coser, et al, *Books: The Culture & Commerce of Publishing* (Basic Books, 1982), and John Tebbel's *Between Covers: The Rise and Transformation of Book Publishing in America* (Oxford, 1987). They too are out of print.

4   Although they make a bundle, the superstores pay most of their employees very little, and provide no benefits—and have thus far fought the workers' drive to unionize, as Michael Moore has told us.

5   Since 1992, moreover, Barnes & Noble has been running its own imprint—publishing, for sale on its own premises, reprints that are underselling Barnes & Noble's suppliers.

6   Likewise, Carol Felsenthal's very thorough *Power, Privilege and* The Post: *The Katherine Graham Story* was heavily attacked by Graham's influential coterie when Putnam publishes it in 1993. (Despite her anger over it, Graham seems to have relied on Felsenthal's biography in researching her *Personal History*—which also fails to mention Felsenthal.) *Power, Privilege and* The Post is out of print.

7 In the UK, Newhouse owns Chatto & Windus, The Bodley Head, Jonathan
   Cape, Century, Hutchinson, Pimlico, Legend, Arrow Books and Ebury
   Press, and will soon buy Heinemann, Secker & Warburg, Methuen, Sinclair
   Stevenson, Mandarin and Minerva.

David Lieberman

CONGLOMERATES, NEWS, AND CHILDREN

The biggest media mergers of the last few years were, to a large degree, responses to tectonic changes in the Hollywood entertainment economy. The core market, the United States, is saturated. In addition, technologies, such as satellites, coaxial cable, and microprocessors enable deep-pocketed new competitors to challenge the relatively small field of entertainment giants led by Time Warner, Disney, Viacom, and News Corp.

But these studios, and other media companies, believe they know how to keep growing. They are launching high-risk efforts to broadcast their productions into new markets overseas, and expand into new entertainment-related businesses. Mergermania helped these efforts by addressing strategic weaknesses—not by building on strengths.

Strangely enough, these plans are fueling a global boom in news and children's entertainment. These are the two forms of programming that media powers used to neglect—because they were only marginally profitable—even though they have the greatest impact on the public.

This article will look at the business rationale for these efforts to appeal to news viewers and kids around the world, and explore some of the questions that they raise for the public interest.

One observation may help to put the recent changes in the media business into perspective: The Tinseltown moguls, who usually look so mighty, are terrified. The main problem is that Disney, Time Warner, Viacom, and Seagram each collect at least 65 percent of their revenues in the United States. And this market is, economically speaking, mature.

We've run out of time for media. The people who measure these things say the average American already devotes nearly 9 hours a day to activities like watching TV or a movie, listening to radio, rummaging the Internet, or reading a newspaper, book, or magazine. That figure has been relatively stagnant for years. There's no sign that it will dramatically change in the near future.

We're also running out of spare cash. Communications giants recently have grown not by expanding their audience but by raising prices. That trend seems to have run its course, though. Unit sales of movie tickets, video rentals, and even cable television subscriptions noticeably slows whenever they ask consumers to dig deeper into their pockets.

It shouldn't be surprising. The Department of Commerce reports that median family incomes, adjusted for inflation, have fallen 7 percent since 1989. Home equity values are stagnant in most of the country. And baby boomers, now entering their fifties, must save both for retirement and their children's college educations. Tuition prices are rising far faster than the inflation rate.

Meanwhile, production costs in movie and TV production are rising far faster than revenues. As a result, studios barely make money on new films. Industry-wide profit margins plummeted from about 11 percent in 1992 to 3 percent in 1995—and they're even lower today. Simply put, studios would collect higher returns by investing their cash into a passbook savings account instead of the silver screen.

Wall Street is catching on. Entertainment company stocks collectively appreciated a mere 2 percent in 1996, while the market enjoyed one of the greatest booms in its history. In addition to the industry-wide problems, investors are nervous about many Hollywood giants because they are groaning under billions in debt. Even before Time Warner bought Turner Broadcasting System, it was America's most indebted company—it owes $17.5 billion to bankers and bond holders. To reduce this burden, companies such as Time Warner and Viacom are struggling to sell some of their operations.

Not so long ago, the studios and networks might have been able to adjust to these changes. They were oligopolies. To protect their profits, they could have just decided (independently, of course) to make fewer or less expensive movies and TV shows.

But times have changed. Aided by new technologies and relatively easy access to capital, the old-line Hollywood studios are in a battle for market share against potent new rivals. For example, there's Holland's PolyGram and DreamWorks SKG—the production company cofounded by director Steven Spielberg. And instead of three over-the-air networks, we now have six—plus more than 100 cable networks.

Media companies not only grapple with new competitors in their core businesses. They also are struggling to keep up with new media. TV programmers shiver at some of the studies they see about what happens when people buy computers and connect to the Internet.

A recent report from Forrester Research predicts that by the year 2001 total viewing hours for the major networks will fall by 5 percent, and for cable networks by 6 percent as one-time couch potatoes become mouse potatoes. Forrester calls the PC "a cancer that will eat away at the vital audiences of established media."

Intel CEO Andy Grove echoed that theme. He told a computer convention in 1996 that his chip-making company is in a war against television for eyeballs. Intel's market value, at about $96 billion, is about twice as big as the most highly valued traditional studio—which is Disney, at $48 billion. And the market puts a price tag of about $90 billion on Microsoft, which now calls itself a media company.

Phone companies also are getting into showbiz. U.S. West just became the third largest cable operator, and it could soon become the country's largest—surpassing Tele-Communications Inc., which has nearly 14 million customers. This is the same TCI that almost sold itself to Bell Atlantic in 1994. Meanwhile, long-distance giant AT&T made a major investment in satellite broadcaster DirecTV. Despite its well-publicized troubles in its core long-distance business, AT&T's market value is still 24 percent higher than Disney. So giants like Time Warner, Disney, News Corp. and Viacom aren't just competing with each other. They are up against rich companies from other industries.

And, in their struggle to hang on to market share, they have produced an entertainment glut. You may sense this yourself on a weekend when you think about going to a movie. We face an average of four new Hollywood productions every weekend. That number rises dramatically during the summer and Christmas seasons, and when you throw in independent and foreign films. During the winter holidays in late 1996, Hollywood released a record sixty-one films—up from fifty-two in 1995. That's nearly seven each weekend.

We may enjoy having so many options, but it's creating havoc for the studios. If a movie isn't a success right away, theaters yank it to make way for a new film that might attract more ticket buyers. The top films in 1995 played for an average of three fewer weeks than the top films did in 1990.

If a film flops in the theaters, then it's usually dead. It probably will also flop on videocassette, which typically accounts for more than half of a film's revenues. And then it will bomb in the broadcast market, where TV stations and basic cable channels want to rent hits.

The average film costs about $60 million to make and market. It's hard to think of any other business that so routinely risks so much money with such unpredictable and narrow opportunities to make the investment pay off.

To minimize these dangers, studios do everything they can to grab our attention. This is one reason studios pay movie stars such as Jim Carrey and Arnold Schwarzenegger more than $20 million to appear in a film. It's not because they're such great actors. It's because they're already well-known, well-liked, and generate lots of free publicity by appearing on magazine covers and TV shows. Audiences may or may not like their films—but at least they'll be aware of them.

Marketing expenses for some big releases can run as high as the production itself. About a decade ago, studios rarely advertised on national television. Now they're collectively one of the top five buyers of TV time. They spent close to $2 billion in 1995, up nearly 39 percent from 1994.

(The biggest beneficiary, by the way, is NBC. Its Thursday night hits—such as *Seinfeld* and *E.R.*—command the highest ad rates on TV, close to $1 million a minute. Studios need to run their spots on the night when many people make their weekend plans.)

The competition to grab our attention is just as tough in television. Only nine of the forty-two new series introduced last year on ABC, CBS, NBC, and Fox even survived to this season. The 1996–97 season began with forty new prime time shows. None has excited viewers enough to qualify as a hit.

To break through the din, networks also are paying more than ever for new shows with major stars. This season's big moneymakers include Bill Cosby, Ted Danson and Mary Steenburgen, and Michael J. Fox. ABC promised to pay $900,000 an episode for a comedy with Arsenio Hall. These programs will probably be what retailers call "loss leaders." They'll lose money, but—with any luck—draw customers to the store.

No wonder, then, that many Hollywood executives are so frightened. A lot of moguls feel like they're stuck in the second reel of last summer's hit movie *Independence Day*. They're watching their power centers get blown up.

Yet, they believe they know a way out of this mess.

First, Hollywood is excited by new opportunities around the globe for them to broadcast their own movies and TV shows on advertiser-supported TV channels. Parts of Europe, Latin America, and Asia are in the midst of an economic boom. There's a burgeoning middle class in countries such as Brazil, Argentina, India, Malaysia, and China.

What's more, many of these countries also began to enjoy a media revolution after the Cold War ended and satellites lowered the cost of entry for new broadcasters. Nations that had lived for years with just a handful of TV channels—most of them government controlled—now have dozens of alternatives via satellite and cable. Consumers also are just starting to go to the multiplex theaters and full-service video stores to which we've already become accustomed.

The most dramatic changes are taking place in Asia—which accounts for more than 30 percent of all the televisions in the world. Cable and satellite penetration is expected to double in China, South Korea, and the Philippines by the year 2001 and grow rapidly in Hong Kong, Singapore, and India.

In 1990, advertisers spent about $19 billion on TV in such major markets as Japan, South Korea, and Australia. By the year 2005, it's expected to hit $57 billion. In short, the market will have tripled in just fifteen years.

China is the biggest market of all with 1.2 billion people. About 73 percent of all homes in China have television sets. The potential TV audience is already more than four times larger than the U.S. This is a breathtaking phenomenon. Up until 1992, television was largely confined to the coastal urban areas around Beijing, Shanghai, and Guangdong. But the market is growing so fast, these three regions now account for just a third of the money spent on TV throughout China.

The next most promising market after China is India. Only 31 percent of the country's 884 million people have televisions. That figure is expected to grow by about 15 percent a year as more remote areas get electricity. As a result, TV advertising should more than double by the year 2001—to $766 million. A lot of that will go to satellite broadcasters, who entered the market in 1992.

For the media giants, then, new overseas channels create fresh opportunities to collect cash from advertisers. And the studios don't have to develop program schedules from scratch. They already have libraries filled with movies and TV shows. They're mostly generating new revenues out of depreciated assets.

These channels can also open additional opportunities for the studios to expand. They now understand that they aren't just in the business of selling TV advertising, cable subscriptions or movie tickets.

Consumers around the world flock to buy products that are emblematic of American culture. Toy stores, clothing stores, book stores, record stores, software stores, fast food restaurants, and theme parks offer a Magic Kingdom of merchandise based on movie and TV stories and characters. Homer Simpson, Bugs Bunny, Pocahontas, and Beavis and Butt-Head constitute what Hollywood calls "intellectual property."

Here's where we can begin to see why nearly every studio is so determined to expand its news and family entertainment operations. They are two of only four programming genres that appeal to audiences around the world. And they are more predictable and adaptable than the other two: hit movies and sports.

The problem with movies is that nobody really knows in advance which ones will be successful. Just ask all the studios that originally passed on *Star Wars, Raiders of the Lost Ark, Home Alone,* and *Back to the Future.* And it is particularly hard to find film genres that appeal to everyone. Moviegoers in Germany love slapstick comedies, such as Mel Brooks films and Leslie Nielsen's *Naked Gun.* But these productions usually bomb in Japan.

The closest thing to a sure-fire worldwide success—besides a Disney cartoon—is an action film featuring a star like Arnold Schwarzenegger or Mel Gibson. Kevin Costner's *Waterworld* cost about $170 million to make and then was a huge disappointment here in the United States. But it made a profit after worldwide revenues rolled in.

As for sports, people around the world love them—but they don't all love the same sport. Just try to find the basketball fans in India, or the rugby fans here. There's a reason why *Sports Illustrated* doesn't have an international edition.

But news and family entertainment don't have these drawbacks—and have some unique attractions.

Let's look first at news.

Viewers around the globe want to know what's happening in their communities and in the world. News services, particularly, grab the attention of educated elites—the people who often decide which companies they want to invite into their countries. News also has broad appeal because producers can easily edit the video to suit local interests.

CNN has demonstrated the universality of news. The channel is seen in more than 210 countries. NBC News is catching up. It already serves forty-four countries in Europe through the network's ownership of Super Channel, the continent's largest general-programming service. MSNBC is due to expand there in late 1997. NBC also has a major news channel in Latin America and is pushing into Asia through NBC Asia and CNBC Asia. And Murdoch's Fox News Channel plans to expand to Latin America, Asia, and Europe by end of 1997. It may air in Macau before it appears in Manhattan.

News helps media companies to enter new markets, and often can succeed as a stand-alone business. Smart distributors, though, look for opportunities to package news channels with other services that offer family entertainment. This is what turns the overseas expansion plan into a potential gold mine.

There's no great mystery here. Parents around the world need a rest once in a while. And—for better or worse—they can get it by plopping their kids in front of the television. The number of tired parents is bound to grow: birth rates worldwide were up 10 percent in 1995. No wonder Rupert Murdoch calls children's TV a "key driver of distribution platforms around the world."

Within the genre of family entertainment, cartoons are the most— to use one of the industry's favorite new buzzwords—"portable." Talking mice, rabbits, ducks, and dogs don't have a nationality - and their voices are easily overdubbed. The recognition of this fact has led to an animation boom.

Disney has nearly 2,000 film animators, up from a few hundred in the mid-1980s. There are now film versions of *Hercules* for summer 1997, followed by *Tarzan* in 1998, and *Fantasia* in 1999. Disney's also expanding by making animated features for videocassette that never appear in the theaters. The latest was a sequel to *Aladdin*, called *Aladdin and The King of Thieves*. This made-for-video movie took a lot of Disney-watchers by surprise. It sold six million copies in the first five days it was on the shelves. In other words, by the end of the first week, Disney had already made a $60 million profit from the film. The company plans to develop sequels to hit films, including *The Lion King* and *Pocahontas*, as made-for-video films.

One of the big questions in Hollywood now is whether Disney is successful because it's so good or because it has had no real competition. We're about to learn the answer. Warner Bros. just revived its feature film animation division, hiring 460 artists. They released *Space Jam* in late 1996 and are planning a movie called *Quest for Camelot*. DreamWorks recently hired about 350 animators to work on four films. The first one—due Thanksgiving 1998—will musically tell the story of Moses' exodus from Egypt. Fox also wants to get into the cartoon business. It hired hundreds of animators to work on a feature film, *Anastasia*.

And in television, Viacom—which owns the children's cable channel Nickelodeon—is about to become one of the largest producers of animated shows. It recently announced plans to spend $420 million over the next five years to produce 850 half-hour animated TV shows.

It's not just the huge studios who are trying to cash in. Independent producers who made high-quality children's fare through the fallow years seem to believe that the future looks promising. Britt Allcroft, the woman responsible for public television's *Shining Time Station*, just took her tiny company public. So did Film Roman, the company that animates *The Simpsons, Garfield & Friends, Felix the Cat, The Critic,* and *The Mask.*

(Incidentally, you could almost pack a whole portfolio with children's entertainment stocks. Fox Kids is about to go public. Lancit Media is built around its PBS show, *Puzzle Place.* Cinar, a Canadian firm, specializes in nonviolent cartoons such as *The Busy World of Richard Scarry.* And Harvey Entertainment has *Casper the Friendly Ghost* and *Richie Rich.*)

The market for children's programming is there. The productions are coming. Now the big fight is over who will control the international distribution channels.

Ted Turner's Cartoon Network—owned by Time Warner—jumped out ahead of the pack by going global shortly after it was launched in the United States in 1992. It broadcasts in ten languages to over seventy-five countries. The Flintstones not only speak English, they are fluent in Spanish, French, Dutch, Portuguese, Swedish, Finnish, Czech, Mandarin, and Thai.

Viacom's Nickelodeon is trying to catch up. It's in Europe; it's exploring Asia; and it will be in Argentina, Brazil, and Mexico by year's end.

Last month, Rupert Murdoch's Fox Kids Network began serving the United Kingdom and announced plans to broadcast to Latin America.

The media powers may face some interesting competition. Children's Television Workshop is thinking about using its twenty-seven-year-old library of hit children's shows—notably *Sesame Street*—to launch a channel tentatively called New Kids City. Planners are looking at potential opportunities in Australia, France, Germany, Spain, and Italy. And The Discovery Channel recently introduced Discovery Kids in Latin America.

Each of these companies shares the view that their programming can become essential marketing platforms for a broad array of consumer goods. A few statistics illustrate what's at stake:

In 1995, parents in the United States and Canada spent more than $16 billion on merchandise based on animated characters. So even without including overseas sales, it's a much bigger business than radio broadcasting or recorded music. Sales keep growing. Ten years ago, only about 10 percent of the toys sold in the United States were based on movie or TV characters. Now over half are tied-in to programming.

And this isn't just a U.S. phenomenon. World sales of toys and games should come in at around $70 billion this year. Revenues are expected to increase 20 percent by the year 2000, according to a recent report from market analyst Euromonitor.

These sales already contribute to Hollywood's bottom line:

- Warner Bros.' three *Batman* films generated more than $4 billion in retail sales of tie-in merchandise. As a rule of thumb, the studio collects about 15 percent of these sales. So, on the back of the envelope, Warner probably collected some $600 million in profit.

- The studio's Looney Tunes characters—led by Bugs Bunny and Daffy Duck—generate about $3 billion in worldwide merchandise retail sales per year.

- Saban Entertainment's *Mighty Morphin Power Rangers* has garnered more than $2 billion in retail sales since 1993.

- Disney—which has the sales process down to an art—derived about 18 percent of its 1995 revenues from consumer products. A decade earlier, this category only contributed 7 percent.

It's a remarkable machine. You may have read about the disappointing ticket sales for Disney's big animated release this summer, *The Hunchback of Notre Dame*. Even so, it will probably end up generating more profit than hotter films such as *Independence Day, Mission: Impossible*, and *Twister*. Disney is expected to earn as much as $450 million in profits from *Hunchback* after all of the merchandise and other worldwide sales are thrown in.

The company, and its investors, were frustrated because its performance didn't match *The Lion King*. That film is estimated to have sold $300 million worth of tickets at movie theaters in the United States, another $400 million overseas, then $650 million in sales of the video, and finally a whopping $1 billion in merchandise. It produced terrific ratings in November 1996 for ABC. It has been spun off into a weekly cartoon series featuring the characters Timba and Pumba. Now the film is going to come back to life as a Broadway production.

Disney is the master of cross-promotion—but others are catching up. Look at what Time Warner did in 1996 with *Space Jam*. The film was profitable at the box office. Time Warner predicted a bonanza, though, from the $1 billion in merchandise sales that might flow from the movie. Not surprisingly, the company is doing everything possible to promote the new franchise. Here's an example of synergy in action:

- The company produced a *Space Jam* soundtrack on its Atlantic Records label.

- *Sports Illustrated's* spin-off magazine, *SI for Kids*, produced a special *Space Jam* issue.

- Time Warner lined up an estimated $50 million in advertising support from corporate sponsors creating tie-ins and other promotional items. The list includes McDonald's, General Mills, and Kraft General Foods.

- The company aired promotional programs for *Space Jam* on the Turner-owned Cartoon Network and other TBS outlets, and mentioned it frequently during TBS' National Basketball Association games.

- The WB network started calling its affiliates "Official *Space Jam* Stations." It may air a spinoff TV series.

- A new Warner Bros. toys unit is making most of the *Space Jam* toys. And more than 100 domestic and 150 international merchandising partners will be selling the products.

Analysts speak metaphorically about entertainment companies needing "shelf space" for their movies and TV shows. But in the case of consumers goods, you need real shelves and real space. Disney understood this when it opened the first Disney Store in 1987. Today there are 530 around the world. Warner cut the ribbon on its first studio store in 1991, and now has 150 around the world.

If you doubt that these outlets are important, take a walk down Fifth Avenue in New York City at 57th Street. You'll see the flow of tourists packing into the Warner Studio Store. Then, at 55th Street, you'll hit the Disney store, with similar lines of products. Hang a left and you'll hit Sony's store.

Other studios are now racing to catch up. A lot of analysts believe that Viacom—which owns the Paramount studio and MTV—could quickly become a powerful retailer of company-related goods through its Blockbuster video stores. As of early August 1996 there were 4,800 Blockbusters worldwide, including 1,450 overseas with recent openings in Scandinavia, Chile, Argentina, Australia, and Italy. In 1997, Viacom will open an average of two new Blockbusters every day—450 domestically and 250 overseas.

It's an extraordinary operation. Here in the States, Blockbuster has 64 million members in 50 percent of total U.S. households. These stores are within three miles of 65 percent of the population. And Blockbuster's database can target customers using up to eighty distinct attributes. At the risk of sounding Orwellian, they know what you rent.

In addition to retailing, hit children's shows help to boost attendance at theme parks. Once again, Disney has shown how the model works. And once again, there's growing competition from Seagram's Universal Studio parks, Viacom's Paramount Parks, and the Six Flags parks affiliated with Time Warner.

Now we can see why the major media companies were so eager to make their deals. Disney was already a powerful producer of family-oriented movies and TV shows—and it dominated the theme park business. But until it bought Capital Cities/ABC, Disney did not have a major TV news operation or channels with the global reach of ESPN. With these assets in the company portfolio, Disney is launching a sports news channel, ESPNews. It's looking for international alliances for ABC News, although the company backed away from launching a separate general news channel. The family-oriented Disney Channel is expanding into the Middle East and France and cultivating its existing Disney channels in the United Kingdom, Taiwan, and Australia. And Disney is drawing up plans to create a cable channel for preschoolers tentatively called ABZ.

There's a similar pattern with Time Warner. It was already Hollywood's most prolific producer of family movies and TV shows. In addition, the company owns the country's second biggest collection of cable franchises, the biggest collection of mass audience magazines, and the biggest recorded music company. But until Time Warner bought Ted Turner's company it didn't have an international TV news operation on the order of CNN or ad-supported entertainment channels like The Cartoon Network and TNT. Now the combined companies are expanding their news roster. CNN has spun off a new sports news service, CNN/SI, and a financial channel, CNNFN. Meanwhile, Time Warner is creating an international family entertainment service called WBTV and is preparing to introduce a premium channel, HBO Family.

Rupert Murdoch's News Corp. has a studio, newspapers, book publishing, and a major TV network. Unlike Disney and Time Warner, he distributes more channels overseas than anyone else—mostly via satellite. But he didn't have a TV news operation in the United States and didn't make children's programming. Ted Turner made sure Murdoch couldn't buy CNN, so he made the investment to create his Fox News Channel. And he forged a partnership with Saban Entertainment—the maker of *Mighty Morphin Power Rangers*—to create an international programming service called Fox Kids.

It may sound as though the media giants have everything figured out. But they don't. Their new strategies are expensive and risky. Even Bill Gates—who can shape the future as much as any executive—had to rewrite more than a third of his book, *The Road Ahead*, in the year between its original release and the new paperback edition. The moguls who guided the last several years of mergermania are simply making bets. Many of the major studios could lose billions.

For starters, there's no guarantee that the economic boom overseas will continue. A crash or major recession in key markets could be devastating.

But even if these markets sustain their growth rates, studios understand that they must spend a lot to market and distribute their programs and products in lots of different countries. Movie distributors, for example, can't reach all of their potential customers in a market by advertising on a few TV stations. The proliferation of broadcast outlets has fragmented audiences.

And local laws or business customers usually prevent studios from doing everything themselves and reaping all of the profits: More often than not Hollywood must forge partnerships with politically powerful local media barons.

Meanwhile, many overseas governments want to hold back the tidal wave of American entertainment. China's Ministry of Radio, Film, and Television only allows 15 percent of its prime-time TV programming to come from overseas suppliers. The agency is developing cable television as fast as it can to slow the spread of foreign-owned satellite services. Shanghai now has the world's largest cable franchise.

It's no wonder, then, that our seemingly all-powerful media giants look like mere paper tigers in Asia. Rupert Murdoch's Star TV satellite service in Asia is still deeply in the red. When the Chinese government objected to news broadcasts from the BBC, Murdoch quickly pulled them off of Star. NBC also seemed to put business ahead of principle in July. The network apologized after sportscaster Bob Costas briefly mentioned during the Olympics that China had "problems with human rights (and) property rights disputes."

Disney recently found itself in the hot seat. Beijing objects to a Disney film called *Kundun* which paints a sympathetic portrait of the Tibet independence movement and its spiritual leader, the Dalai Lama. Disney has said it will still distribute *Kundun*, even if China tries to shut out the studio's other productions. That could be a serious blow to Disney. Its characters already are big sellers—Disney toys and tee-shirts are popular throughout the country. Just recently, the studio's film *Toy Story* sold $1.2 million worth of tickets when it played for just one month in one city, Shanghai.

But even in areas where governments let new channels in, competitors may create bottlenecks. We don't have to look far to see how that works. Studios became determined to buy or start networks here in the United States to ensure that rivals couldn't keep their products off the airwaves. That would be a serious blow. Most movies and TV shows must succeed here before they even have a chance of making it abroad. We're the world's Good Housekeeping Seal of Approval.

This helps to explain the vicious war between Murdoch and Time Warner—particularly its new Vice Chairman Ted Turner. Time Warner owns the cable system in Manhattan. It is a key outlet for new cable channels because it serves the Madison Avenue advertising community.

So it was a terrible blow to Murdoch's ambition to launch a global news channel when Time Warner decided to carry MSNBC—but not the Fox News Channel. Murdoch retaliated by scuttling a deal with Time Warner involving his satellite service BSkyB, which controls the multichannel TV market in Great Britain. BSkyB was supposed to begin broadcasting Warner's new family entertainment service, called WBTV, to its 3 million subscribers there.

Another potential threat comes from all of the local producers of movies and TV shows. They know their audiences a lot better than we do—even if they can't always match our big budget special effects and overall pizzazz.

Hollywood's historic competitive advantage may be less secure than we'd like to believe. Microprocessors are becoming so powerful that anyone with a few off-the-shelf personal computers soon will be able to duplicate the special effects that thrilled audiences when *Star Wars* was released in 1977.

Computers, particularly, lower the cost of animation. Japan is already a net exporter of cartoons. And China Central Television, the national network, recently installed a state-of-the-art computerized animation facility capable of cranking out forty minutes of programming a month.

Here's one other frightening thought. What if the animation boom turns out to be short-lived? Remember, the cartoon business nearly became extinct between the mid-1960s and the 1980s. Disney lost $40 million in 1985 with a feature-length cartoon called *The Black Cauldron*. The business came back to life three years later when Disney scored back-to-back hits with *Who Framed Roger Rabbit?* and *The Little Mermaid*.

So, we've seen that Hollywood wants news and children's entertainment that will appeal to audiences around the world. We've seen that they also want to make profits from new businesses, like retailing and theme parks. And we've seen that they want to be vertically integrated—to produce and distribute their programs—as a strategy to avoid hostile gatekeepers.

There's still one more component to their new plans: branding. Most major global companies try to presell you their wares—and stand out from the crowd—by developing reputations. You know what to expect in advance when you hear a brand name like McDonald's, Coca-Cola, and Calvin Klein.

This concept applies to news. On election night—or when there's a crisis—television viewers don't start shopping for a reliable newscast. They already know whether they want Peter Jennings, Dan Rather, Tom Brokaw, or Bernard Shaw.

Branding can sell a genre of entertainment. Since 1966 Paramount's *Star Trek* franchise has expanded to four prime-time TV series, eight movies, a Saturday morning animated series, 65 million books in 15 languages, and over $1 billion in merchandise sales.

Now that concept is being applied to entertainment company names. Disney has become a brand name for a level of quality in family entertainment. Fox is trying to establish itself as a brand for fast-paced and edgy fare. There's a reason why its channels are named Fox Sports, Fox News, and Fox Kids. If they establish a music video channel, two guesses what it will be called. The other studios also are sharpening their brand identities. Seagram, for example, is preparing to rename its entertainment operation Universal Studios, and drop the more oblique corporate title MCA.

Okay, so now what does all of this mean for the public interest?

This is tough to answer for just the reason that Pat Aufderheide will raise: There's no consensus on how to define the public interest in the new media environment. For years, advocates of quality television have asked, even begged, media moguls to offer more, better, and more diverse news and children's fare. Now we're starting to get it both on broadcast TV and on cable.

The major networks and their stations—including Fox—are beefing up their news operations. NBC started a news channel, MSNBC. Meanwhile, CBS bought a Spanish language international news channel, Telenoticias, and plans to launch a personality-oriented news and information cable service called Eye on People.

Meanwhile, kids shows air weekday afternoons on PBS, Fox, UPN, and the WB networks. ABC and CBS join in on weekends. On cable, children have options on thirteen networks including The Disney Channel, The Learning Channel, Nickelodeon, and the Cartoon Network.

In the overworked phrase from the presidential campaign, we're better off now than we were four years ago.

The interesting question is: How long will this last? Much of the new programming we're seeing is subsidized research and development. If there's no payoff, then many of these ventures will die. And the odds look daunting. Unless the market grows substantially, then more competition means more audience fragmentation. When ratings fall, so does advertising support. That means there's less cash available.

A shakeout could leave us with a paradoxical situation: More choices, and less diversity. This may sound absurd. Microsoft's Bill Gates, for example, envisions endless diversity as computer users connect to the Internet and broadcast their views to the world.

But while talk is cheap, news isn't. You need millions to pay for reporters, international bureaus, and long-term investigations. If the money isn't there, you can either cheapen the product or amortize your expenses by dominating lots of different markets.

NBC understands this process. Its news appears on a national broadcast network, two cable channels, a video service that goes to business computers, an Internet site, and a fast-growing collection of channels around the world. Here's a case where we have more choices for getting news, but not much more diversity of viewpoints. If NBC has an institutional blind spot to a certain kind of story, it will cross all of these outlets.

We can see the same phenomenon in children's entertainment. High-quality animated TV shows often are more expensive to produce than most prime-time sitcoms. Yet they attract a small fraction of the audience. So we'll have more choices as cartoon characters leap from movies to videos, TV shows, records, Broadway shows, ice shows, CD-ROMs, and more merchandise than any of us can imagine. But if there's a shakeout in the business, most of these choices will be provided by just a few companies like Disney.

It would be easy to find grounds to object if the market once again becomes an oligopoly. But other developments will raise more troublesome questions. Even now we might ask ourselves: How should we feel about this deafening din of marketing messages designed to attract consumer dollars?

Don't jump to easy conclusions.

As a parent of a young child, I'm glad to see the renaissance of quality family entertainment and classically inspired movies like *The Lion King* and *Pocahontas*. They are beautifully drawn and lavishly orchestrated. And if Disney goes ahead with its plan to replace ABC's current Sunday night shows with a *Disney Family Movie*—that would be good news in my household. We are not fans of *America's Funniest Home Videos*. My daughter will probably remember Disney's productions—and other new productions—as fondly as I remember *Bambi*, *Dumbo* and *Mary Poppins* and spending Sunday nights in front of the TV watching Disney's *Wonderful World of Color*.

Someone has to pay for this.

But, yes, I am worried that our culture will be overwhelmed by the ceaseless barrage of marketing firepower. Disney was even able to quantify its marketing reach before it acquired Capital Cities/ABC. Former company President, Michael Ovitz, said, in January 1996, that "a project of any sort promoted by Disney has the ability to reach 375-to-425 million consumer contacts in any three-month period. 375-to-425 million consumer contacts going through our parks, visiting our stores, seeing our films and television programs, watching our videos, playing our games, hearing our music, or visiting our Internet sites." ABC, he added, "only adds to the ability geometrically."

It's one thing to make good programming possible. It's another to make it inescapable. What's more, this hypermarketing could drown out alternatives from producers who either can't or won't turn their shows into long-form commercials for a department-store's worth of licensed goods.

So one question to be addressed in any redefinition of the public interest: Who should pay for the good stuff?

Right now public television offers some relief from these pressures. It doesn't run commercials, and its children's programming is often terrific. But it still serves as a vehicle for brand creation and promotion.

The company that produces one of PBS's most popular new kids shows—*Puzzle Place*—is struggling because toys and games based on the show aren't selling as well as expected. Now the company is trying to relaunch the program and boost merchandise sales. *Puzzle Place* characters will be promoted by Kix cereal, and they will appear in a live show that will tour the country's shopping malls.

Of course, there are plenty of alternatives on cable or videocassette. But that brings us to another troublesome issue: the gap between the culture and information haves and the have-nots. It's already wide. The number of people who own computers in the United States is just about the same as the number of people who don't even subscribe to cable television.

Who, if anyone, is responsible for closing the gap? This one will be tough to answer. Despite the gallant efforts by some schools and libraries to democratize media, just about every trend in the marketplace suggests that the gap will continue to widen.

Consider a few ways this could happen:

- What if NBC wanted to run its election night news coverage on MSNBC, and air more profitable sitcoms on the over-the-air network?

- Imagine that Disney concluded that it could make more money on the Super Bowl or the World Series by airing it on ESPN instead of ABC?

- And here's one not-so-imaginary scenario: CBS is having a terrible time this season with its Saturday morning children's shows. Ratings are down by 45 percent as lots of kids switch to cable channels like Nickelodeon. Now the network has decided to cancel most of its Saturday morning children's programming. It will just offer the bare minimum that the federal government requires: three hours of educational fare.

Many people might be outraged at these developments. One third of the country would have fewer opportunities to enjoy sports, news, and children's entertainment. But is there a right to have them free of charge?

Maybe there is. Government officials and public interest advocates have long insisted that they can make special demands on broadcasters in exchange for their use of the public airwaves. The problem is, most viewers—and the marketplace—don't make the same distinctions. CBS does compete with Nickelodeon.

Should the government redefine this to make public interest demands on all television broadcasters—including cable? There's some new ground being broken here. Before the Federal Trade Commission approved Time Warner's deal to buy Turner Broadcasting, the agency insisted that Time Warner carry an all-news competitor to CNN. Public interest advocates, such as the Consumers Union and the Consumer Federation of America, applauded the FTC's move.

But the FTC had to define what it meant, and that has generated some controversy. The agency said that Time Warner had to carry an advertiser-supported news-sports-and-weather channel. That clearly meant either MSNBC or Fox News. The FTC apparently would not have accepted C-SPAN, CNBC, or a political channel like the conservative National Empowerment Television as acceptable alternatives. C-SPAN is now challenging the ruling as a violation of the First Amendment.

These questions don't begin to cover all of the public interest questions that flow from the changes taking place in media. They simply illustrate a few of the directions that this debate could take.

There is no better time to have the discussions that could produce a new understanding of the media giants' obligations to the public. Even most moguls no longer accept the view—so fashionable in the 1980s—that the public interest is served by whatever programming interests the public. It's not that they have become fans of Ralph

Nader. They just know that the callous old view can lead them to do things that tarnish the brand identities they are trying so hard to polish all over the world.

The executives who run today's media powers are neither angels nor demons. They have no blueprints to build Bedford Falls or Potterville. They are nervously stumbling into uncertain, and possibly dangerous, new territory. Like it or not, we will be affected by what they do. It's time for them—and for public interest advocates—to reassess their goals, and discuss ways to address each other's needs through a period of such radical change in the business.

Patricia Aufderheide

TELECOMMUNICATIONS AND THE PUBLIC INTEREST

This is a time of great ideological peaks and valleys. One day the *Nation* tells you with grim foreboding that about seven people will have a stranglehold on your mind from now on, and in fact probably have since last week. The next day *Wired* tells you that the Net is unbounded, beyond government censorship, beyond every possible silly, old-fashioned, tired, old-media kind of paradigm.

This flip-flop between apocalypse and utopia can make you giddy, or drive you to curmudgeonly despair. Unfortunately, either pose, at this moment, is an expensive indulgence. We are, inexorably if ungracefully, lurching away from an era of discrete media—print, film, electronic media—and into an era of communications networks. What had been media is becoming applications, content, and appliances on a communications-transportation infrastructure—an infrastructure that may someday be as pervasive and essential to myriad small acts of our daily lives as it will be invisible.

New paradigm, new possibilities, new realities. One of those realities is not so new, though: the fact that telecommunications provision is an essential part of our daily lives and, as such, a social resource.

As a social resource, it might serve to promote and expand public spaces. This is a concept that involves both reservation of space and creation of content, and it has a long and illustrious history in this country.

Our visionary philosopher John Dewey argued that the public is a set of social relationships that citizens have, allowing them to congregate, discuss, and act on issues that affect them all, especially issues that result from the actions of large institutional forces like government and business (Dewey, 1927). From this perspective, the public interest in communication is served by the permitting and encouraging of spaces and behaviors that promote public interaction and expression, autonomous from industry or government. Call it fostering public life, encouraging public spaces, promoting a civic culture.

We need that concept today as never before. It could help us to breathe new life into the exhausted concept of the public interest in telecommunications, since the old interpretations—never very strong—have broken down with changing regulatory regimes and technological innovation (Horwitz, 1989). Technopundits tell us we need to understand and use the potential of our emerging communications architecture to restore civil connection (Bollier, 1996; Rifkin, 1995; Sclove, 1995).

To revivify the notion of public interest in telecommunications, we need to start by turning down the noise from all the doomsaying and cyberbabble out there. But first, let's dispense with a crippling misapprehension: that the major players—the phone companies, the entertainment companies, the cable and satellite and publishing companies—have any idea what they're doing as they face this paradigm shift. It's not an enviable position, being the chief operating officer of a large telephone company, or an electronics company, or a broadcaster, or a publisher these days. These guys can no longer even be sure what business they're in. They're scared to change, and scared not to. It's really no wonder that the stink of fear pervades the industry, that strategies to stave off competition are the most popular, and that Wall Street is jittery toward players it has traditionally seen as the safest of bets.

At this moment of great anxiety, reality is very virtual indeed, and alarmists and enthusiasts of all kinds have great sway. They have purveyed, over the last couple of years, propositions that are like mirror images of each other, and, that added together, paralyze movement toward defining and deploying the public interest in telecommunications.

Monopoly and Competition

While apocalyptics decry the rise of unregulated monopoly, utopians celebrate the imminent arrival of free-for-all competition. Both visions can easily betempered by reality.

The new telecommunications law finally makes legal what has become technically possible: competition in areas that traditionally were considered natural monopolies, such as telephony and cable. There is much to admire in this model. Real competition could bring down prices, spur innovation, expand the market, and relieve regulators and watchdog groups of the painful process of regulating monopolies by rate of return on profit. But theory and reality are far apart in an industry where any competition must be contrived, managed, and monitored (Vietor, 1994).

Competition in any case is a largely unwelcome opportunity for the largest industry players. They have been driven both to accept and to design a competitive future because of potentially profit-sapping encroachments and competition. But let's not forget that it took two decades to write and pass this law precisely because incumbents had such a built-up interest in old-fashioned monopoly and market power.

We can certainly dispense with utopian dreams of rampant and spontaneous competition, at least for the short and middle term. A year after the law was passed, the phone companies had won a reprieve from competition in the local market by getting a court to invalidate the rules the FCC wrote to govern competition. They even invested in a $7 million campaign to educate us about why they need a better deal. Meanwhile, Time Warner has discreetly told investors that it's not that interested in phone service after all, and might be willing to dump its cable interests and all the promised synergy of vertical integration to focus on its core business of content. There are no viable applications from telecommunications companies to offer what's known as "open video service," a virtually regulation-free version of cable TV. Those are just three examples of ways in which corporations are not leaping onto the new playing field.

On the other hand, unregulated monopoly in converged businesses is also unlikely. The law still frowns on monopoly, and big industry players like to use the law when they're threatened. This is, after all, how Rupert Murdoch finds himself complaining to the courts about those suddenly evil monopolists Time Warner, when he's trying to get his Fox News channel on their cable services. It was advertisers, fearful of higher rates, who pushed the Department of Justice to ban radio mergers that would create more than 40 or 50 percent (depending on the place) of the local market. There are also hulking forces on the landscape kicking down the doors of old monopolists, and eager to use policy to that end. British Telecom has not bought MCI in order to have the local phone companies shut them out of the markets they want indefinitely. Finally, abuse of monopoly power leads to consumer revolt and the prospect of government intervention. That's a messy process without any promise that the cure won't be worse than the disease, but it is another check on the power of monopoly.

The big, however, are getting bigger and the small are getting squeezed, as Douglas Gomery regularly reports in his columns in *American Journalism Review.* Small cable owners are declining, pressed by their DBS competitors. Mom-and-pop radio stations are becoming history. In enhanced network services like Internet provision, the name of the game is to launch and sell out. The 1996 telecommunications reform law permitted such unprecedented cross-ownership and concentration of ownership that in broadcasting alone the dealmaking reached $25-plus billion, triple the previous record of the year before. In these deals, the already big got much bigger.

That kind of consolidation looks good to some of the most eager advocates of competition—because they think this new competitive environment will be a "dance of the giants," with room made for little guys in the niches and boutiques at the edges. They need a few more giants to make this kind of competition work. Permitting concentration of megamedia power is one way of growing competitors for the phone companies, and for other global media companies. But megacorporations may very well decline to compete with their mega-siblings, or may find themselves in unexpected alliances with them.

Our middle-range communications future will probably be one of a rather small number of huge, complex corporations, wielding inter-national clout, and making alliances of convenience with each other. Think of it as chaos theory meets oligopoly. This makes a powerful case for the continued role of regulation in maintaining and manag-ing competition. Or, as Eli Noam, a noted savant in this area, has said, "The price of liberalization is eternal vigilance."

Freedom of Expression
A second set of extremist visions has to do with freedom of expres-sion in this new environment. The doomsayers somberly predict the stamping out of alternative voices, while on the other side, people can only see a thousand electronic mailing lists blossoming.

As an editor for a small, stubborn, pathetically underfunded alter-native voice—the newspaper *In These Times*—I have to say that the range of voices is a real but not a new problem. It is, in fact, a variety of problems, some of which are grave without being easy to find clear villains for, like the evolution of consumer appetite for "infotain-ment." Certainly we have more consumer options than in the past, even if most of those options are junk. Only recently there was much less information choice—three television networks provided isomor-phic versions of the news; small-town newspapers whose editors were often hand-in-glove with local politicians ran local info-autocracies; the book publishing universe didn't extend twenty-five miles outside New York City.

Of course, more stuff is not the same thing as stuff from many dif-ferent sources. Consolidation certainly doesn't seem to be doing much for the quality and diversity of news—one time-honored measure of public service and the platforming of public issues in communications. In radio and TV, local news is already too rare a phenomenon, and mergers in broadcasting mean even more business for cheap syndication services like Metro Networks and Shadow Broadcast Services, which provide the illusion of local reporting. Job opportunities for journalists are actually shrinking as mergers precipitate "downsizing." The instant Time Warner merged with Turner, 1,000 jobs disappeared. Synergies within may not correlate with quality. CNN hopes to expand its TV coverage by reusing *Time* reporting; but insiders at *Time* say that making magazine research hostage to TV development schedules has contorted priorities and held up release of topical information. Meanwhile, media consolidation has accelerated a disturbing trend. The cable public affairs service C-SPAN—which started as the cable industry's present to Congress for pro-cable 1984 legislation and since has become a round-the-clock civics lesson for millions—shrank or disappeared for more than five million cable households over the last four years. Cable companies increasingly find they'd rather sell the space, for excellent prices, to channels offered by rising conglomerates like News Corp and Time Warner. And they no longer feel like they need to kiss Congress goodnight.

As well, we know our media magnates are not shy to throw their weight around in editorial meetings. Both Rupert Murdoch (who contributed $1 million to the California Republican Party in fall 1996) and John Malone have been proud to say publicly that they intend to promote conservative political views in media they control. It also is only common sense that offending one's employer is bad business; ABC's progressive radio talk show host Jim Hightower, whose show was summarily cancelled, may have simply pulled low ratings, but it probably didn't help that, after Disney bought ABC, he said things like, "Now I work for a rodent." This problem of gatekeepers' manipulation is also familiar—we have only to revisit the lives of William Randolph Hearst or Philip Graham—and one with imperfect solutions. But the scale is unprecedented. We are reminded, in the showdown between Disney and the Chinese government in late 1996 over the making of a film about Tibet, that global companies have not only global impact but global sensitivities.

The issue of information integrity when it's an element in corporate synergy or partnering is a perennial problem that has, with the 1996 Act, attained breathtaking new dimensions. Consider recent items in *Columbia Journalism Review*'s "Synergy Watch" column, which tracks effects of concentration on information. It notes an advertisers' breakfast hosted by *The New Yorker*, which celebrated both an upcoming issue and a book published by another arm of its corporate parent; a canny insertion of Rupert Murdoch's Sky News service into the Rupert-owned Fox movie *Independence Day*; and electronic city guides run by software companies, which could weaken newspapers' advertising base and thus threaten the financial health of local news. The potential for crossover marketing and shaping of info-agendas is mind-boggling.

As long as we have gatekeepers—and they're not going away, since gatekeeping is where the money is—we continue to have very old-fashioned issues about informing the public, which return us to considerations of policy. Consider the Time Warner-Turner merger. The Department of Justice required the merged company to carry at least one other twenty-four-news channel, so that the company couldn't exclude everything but CNN. That was clear evidence of the kind of regulatory micromanagement we'll probably see more of as merged companies develop.

As for a thousand electronic mailing lists blooming, this is the kind of technologically utopian argument that works better if you're not on a lot of mailing lists already. Of course distributed networks change, potentially, the economics of information access. But many factors—the cost of access, the reluctance of media corporations to surrender control over content, and the bedeviling problem of getting an audience—hobble that potential. And even if thousands of info-boutiques bloom, what does that mean for shared understanding, for cultural evolution? Today's reality is markedly experimental, and too many changes need to occur to make any sensible predictions about media in a distributed environment.

Changing paradigms will not change, in other words, very familiar issues relating to gatekeeping. If we pretend we can dispense with policy controls on monopoly, or can shrug off broad (if inchoate) public and parental concern over content control, we will only return to those questions in a more highly-charged atmosphere later.

Access

While pessimists foresee the gap between info-haves and have-nots growing, optimists foresee everyone benefitting from cheaper distribution of information.

Inequality is an issue in any infrastructure; technologies will have whatever effect society and government allows them to have, and inequality by and large needs redress by redistribution. The 1996 telecommunications law recognizes this in small ways, with provisions for a special small business fund, educational technology fund, and special low rates for schools, libraries, and health care facilities. As usual, what this means in real life will have everything to do with how much public scrutiny and pressure is on the regulatory process. It will be fatally easy to reinforce existing inequalities (Wresch, 1996). Furthermore, as new and different fault lines will develop, citizens of entire states, not to mention nations, may suddenly be redistricted into the have-not category as a result of new decisions about censorship, competition, or pricing.

As for seeing information get cheaper, that too depends on calculated political decisions. That is exactly what the phone companies are fighting about when they argue about how much it should cost for another company to hook up to their services and compete with them. (They would like the price to be very high, which would put a serious crimp in any price competition.) That is why the Disney corporate lawyers are leaders in a campaign to extend copyright protection to current holders, which would protect their investment in The Mouse and further keep use of other decades-old material costly for everyone.

But just to look at the kinds of savings you can get today, consider that sometimes cost saving is just cost shifting. You know this if you have ever had to print out a document you downloaded. That is a fact Congress understood all too well when our legislators cut appropriations, in 1996, for hard copy of basic governmental documents to the depository libraries nationwide in favor of electronic versions—trusting that the costs of accessing and printing would be borne by locals.

These and other information-equality issues are tracked by the several public-interest-oriented organizations, including Media Access Project, Digital Future Coalition, and the American Library Association. But they're too often ignored in mainstream journalism. Journalists, in turn, complain that their editors say the subject is too dense. Some conclusions, though, are easy to draw. Cost, as we learned in the breakup of AT&T, will be a direct result of policy decisions that go in tandem with other policy decisions about social inequity and about what constitutes the public domain. And that argues for better, deeper journalistic coverage of the nexus between government regulation and industry structure. This, of course, is exactly what one doesn't expect to see on *Entertainment Tonight*, and it's a little hard to imagine an editor employed in megamedia seizing upon the opportunity without pressure. The valiant boutique-information providers of journalism magazines, Internet newsletters, and action alerts need alliances with other citizen voices to provide that pressure.

Deregulation

Has policy become an outmoded tool for citizen activists? Deregulation has cut the public out of decision making, says one side. Don't worry, says the other, regulators were part of the problem, and we're better off without them. Both sides indulge in illusions about the magnitude of deregulation, when the real issue is understanding how regulatory paradigms are changing.

If communications has been deregulated, somebody should tell the FCC lawyers who have been sleeping on their couches since February 1996, when the new telecommunications act was passed. True, the new law basically equates competition with the public interest, and says that the FCC should abandon any regulation that impedes competition. At the same time, the FCC is in charge of maintaining many of the old rules—rules for instance that require broadcasters to provide lowcost airtime to electoral candidates, and to air three hours a day of children's TV. Those old-fashioned rules are there and still enforced largely because of pressure by feisty public interest groups such as Media Access Project and the Center for Media Education. These groups recognize that many aspects of our communications structure continue to be old-fashioned, and any public benefits of the emerging regime entirely unproven.

The notion of the public interest is, thus, still alive and being redefined in ongoing policy. The FCC is tackling it in issues ranging from providing for universal telephone service to spectrum auctions to the use of noncommercial reserved space on direct broadcast satellite services. The policy process there is open to public comment, as it is at state Public Service and Public Utilities Commissions, where the future of telephony is being hammered out, and where the Consumer Federation of America and the American Association of Retired Persons have been active for years.

Indeed, the new communications era of networking, as evidenced by the Internet, seems only to have generated new flowcharts full of policy-body acronyms, most of them international. And the challenges of digital transmission to copyright are further proliferating international policy-making bodies.

The challenge facing those concerned with social equity is thus twofold: to understand the fast-changing road map of policy choices, and to offer proposals that can open opportunities and close resource gaps.

Yesterday, Tomorrow, and Today

The giddiness and panic that afflict this field generally also affect any timetable for public action. Apocalyptics think we have to act yesterday, and utopians think we don't have to do anything right now. These may be the most dangerous misconceptions now plaguing discussion. But what is it exactly that what Gramsci called "optimists [of the will]," realists who can still hope, can or should do today?

An always useful thing is to launch and keep open discussion about what is at stake as we design our communications infrastructure. Of course, this is not one issue but, like any infrastructural architecture, a phenomenon that touches many different groups differently. Intellectual property, privacy, open government, educational applications, prices, among many other issues, attract their own constituencies, even as they affect common values and goals, as computer policy expert Steven Miller elegantly maps in terms of recent legislation (Miller, 1996).

One anchor for our thought is the notion of the public sphere as a place where a democratic culture happens. We can ask how communications networks can encourage an active civil society.

As a nation, we have made a sizeable investment in public culture through communications policy in the past. In 1792, Congress decided to free the postal system from its time-honored role as a revenue-raiser (John, 1996). Instead, Congress decided to give postal routes and post offices to any community that requested them, even if it wasn't cost effective. Legislators, of course, promptly lavished them on constituents, rapidly extending the service to the frontier. The Act also subsidized the cheap distribution of newspapers to readers and the exchange of newspapers among printers, by overpricing letter rates.

That made news a cheap, widely available commodity in the new nation. Congress knew what it was doing. The point was to foster civic knowledge about other parts of a widely dispersed nation, and a sense of participation in nationhood. This was a costly decision. By 1832, newspapers made up 95 percent of postal weight but, at most, only 15 percent of revenue. But the policy was so broadly popular, with merchants, printers, and citizens alike, that it quickly established itself as accepted practice.

Public broadcasting is another interesting example of subsidy for public spaces, this time electronic. It's kind of a Little-Engine-That-Could story. The government was persuaded to put aside only a little spectrum, and that a little late, for public uses (McChesney, 1993; Streeter, 1996). The 1967 Public Broadcasting Act was decisive in making public broadcasting into a remarkable force—some people call it "a barker channel for the culture"—even though it simultaneously hobbled public broadcasting to Congressional appropriations (Aufderheide, 1991; Engelman, 1996). Thirty years later, the American public has a billion-dollar investment in public broadcasting, which has a distinctive profile and is represented in more American communities than any other broadcast service.

The embattled history of cable access programming in the United States is another story of the significance of even small public spaces. The public, educational, and government access channels that some communities have required cable companies to offer have been places people turn to for their children's sporting events, board of education meetings, and even sessions of public outrage at moments such as the announcement of the Rodney King verdict (Aufderheide, 1994).

The notion of reserved space or reserved spectrum has been pooh-poohed by utopians as an old-fashioned and outdated concept. But I think it still has a lot to recommend it, partly because our telecom paradigm is still pretty old-fashioned and top-down, and partly because it seems to be an important feature of stimulating or zoning services such that cultures can grow. Certainly the notion of some kind of reserved spectrum—which also has been called "public rights of way on the information superhighway"—has been much discussed, and there are legal precedents for building it into the new paradigm. For instance, an appeals court in 1996 upheld the 1992 Cable Act's requirement that DBS services set aside 4 to 7 percent of their transmission space for nonprofit uses. The Telecommunications Act requires some kind of lower-cost rate—maybe even free access—for telecommunications services for schools and libraries and rural health care facilities. We could also imagine this space being created as a service funded by interest on, say, spectrum auctions.

Our three-decade tradition of funding arts and humanities expression at the local, state, and federal level should not be ignored. Despite continuous, and sometimes rabid, conservative efforts to destroy the NEA and NEH, the organizations survive because of the way in which such expression feeds highly valued noncommercial relationships and public behaviors.

We have living precedents for the creation of public space. In the past, content creation was a critical part of the process, and it will be in any future that has public domains in it. We must, therefore, ask of our communications future more than simple access to cheap services that allow privacy. We need to carve out distinctive space for public life. To do that, we need to point to concrete projects, so that people who are not already in on the story can imagine this. As well, we need some way of participating in policy making to make sure we get it.

What public spaces will look like fifteen years from now will depend to some extent on the shape of the industry, but they will also depend on what people demand from both industry and government. This is a good moment to pursue experiments in electronic public culture that can provoke both ideas and demands. The flourishing of Freenets, those low- or no-cost computer networks available to local citizens, dozens of which now exist across the country, is one early example, as are efforts by access cable centers to become communications nodes (Schuler, 1996). At the Corporation for Public Broadcasting are people who imagine public broadcasting as your local electronic public library of the future. They are funding demonstration projects in "civic networking." Back in more traditional public broadcasting, you can find an impressive example of community building with media in the work of *P.O.V.* This documentary series which shows about ten new documentaries on PBS each summer, uses each broadcast as an opportunity to launch local discussions, debate, and action. The series both signals and promotes new nodes of public life. At the Department of Commerce, a small, perpetually endangered but productive little program called TIIAP funds around $14 million of experiments in public networking. Projects ranging from language training in Native American school systems to telemedicine for people in the rural Southwest to areawide community development planning to job training for poor kids in the city have all taken off with TIIAP funds, which challenge nonprofit organizations to team up together. And the Benton Foundation, an operating foundation dedicated to promoting nonprofit uses of new technologies, has not only established some demonstration projects in electronic public space, but launched discussion platforms. Its Internet site, like that of the Media Access Project, links to those of scores of other nonprofit organizations.

These demonstration projects are only some among many. We need both to celebrate them and to learn what they do and do not do well. It's hard at this moment even to figure out what's being done. That's why a project like FARNET's database is important. FARNET, or the Federation of American Research Networks (it grew out of NSFNet, an early provider of Internet hookup) is building a database of digital networks that deliver local public services.

As we start to assemble a bigger picture, we need to develop critical insight based on that experience, to find out what electronic public space means and can mean. And, if history is any guide, a lot of our pioneering efforts will demonstrate what doesn't work.

Conclusion

Policy, that bigfooted presence of government, will not disappear with megamedia. On the contrary, it will become an ever more potent tool for better and worse, in a highly volatile atmosphere. As the big-money players already know, the United States has the most open policy process in the world (although that's not saying much). But in order to participate, at a minimum, you do have to be informed. Fortunately, an impressive amount of effort and wit are going into citizen education about telecommunications, among just the kinds of organizations that DeTocqueville, so long ago, found quaint and admirable among us: voluntary associations. These are organizations that analyze issues and mobilize constituencies for defense of the public interest, variously defined, in communications—organizations whose interests range from the price of ISDN lines to children's media to intellectual property rights. Their challenge is to explain to other organizations in civil society the issues at stake in telecommunications, and to work with them. That, in fact, is the mandate of the budding organization NetAction.

This is a time of tremendous creativity and tremendous frustration, which, under cultivation and with a little bit of luck, could turn into new possibilities. That, however, will all happen in history, that zone of real life between the all-too-prevalent discourses of apocalypse and utopia.

Note

Conversations with Andrew Blau, Mary Ellen Burns, Lisa Baumgartner, Larry Daressa, Douglas Gomery, Richard John, David Lieberman, Mark McCarthy, Andy Schwartzman, Steve Schwartzman, and Gigi Sohn were particularly helpful in shaping my understanding.

References

AUFDERHEIDE, P. "Public Television and the Public Sphere," *Critical Studies in Mass Communication*, 1991, 168-183.

AUFDERHEIDE, P. "Underground Cable: A Survey of Public Access Programming," *Afterimage*, 22:1 (Summer 1994), 5-7.

BOLLIER, D. "Reinventing Democratic Culture in an Age of Electronic Networks." Report to the John D. And Catherine T. MacArthur Foundation, 1996, Available at http://www.netaction.org.

DEWEY, J. *The Public and Its Problems.* (New York: Holt and Company, 1927).

ENGELMAN, R. *Public Radio and Television in America.* (Thousand Oaks, Calif.: Sage, 1996).

HORWITZ, R. *The Irony of Regulatory Reform.* (New York: Oxford University Press, 1989).

JOHN, R. *Spreading the News.* (Cambridge, Mass.: Harvard, 1995).

MILLER, S. *Civilizing Cyberspace.* (New York: ACM Press, 1996).

MCCHESNEY, R. *Telecommunications, Mass Media and Democracy.* (New York: Oxford University Press, 1993).

RIFKIN, J. *The End of Work.* (New York: Tarcher/Putnam, 1995).

SCHULER, D. *New Community Networks.* (Reading, Mass.: Addison-Wesley, 1996).

SCLOVE, R. *Democracy and Technology.* (New York: Guilford, 1995).

STREETER, T. *Selling the Air.* (Chicago: University of Chicago Press, 1996).

VIETOR, R. *Contrived Competition: Regulation and Deregulation in America.* (Cambridge, Mass.: Harvard University Press, 1994).

WRESCH, W. *Disconnected: Haves and have-nots in the Information Age.* (New Brunswick, N.J.: Rutgers University Press, 1996).

A Pocket Directory of Public Interest Connections on the Net

BENTON FOUNDATION: http://www.benton.org

CENTER FOR MEDIA EDUCATION: http://www.cme.org

COMPUTER PROFESSIONALS FOR SOCIAL RESPONSIBILITY: http://www.cspr.org

MEDIA ACCESS PROJECT: http://www.mediaaccess.org

NETACTION: http://www.netaction.org

AMERICAN JOURNALISM REVIEW Columnist Douglas Gomery:
   dgomery@jmail.umd.edu

COLUMBIA JOURNALISM REVIEW'S SYNERGY WATCH: cjr@columbia.edu

DIGITAL FUTURE COALITION/AMERICAN LIBRARY ASSOCIATION:
   alawash@alawash.org

FEDERAL COMMUNICATIONS COMMISSION: http://www.fcc.gov

CORPORATION FOR PUBLIC BROADCASTING'S CIVIC NETWORKING:
   http://www.cpb.org/civnet

PUBLIC TV PROGRAM *P.O.V.*: http://www.pbs.org/pov

NATIONAL TELECOMMUNICATIONS INFORMATION ADMINISTRATION
   GRANTS PROGRAM: http://www.ntia.gov/doc/tiiap

LIBERATION MARKETING AND THE CULTURE TRUST

Anybody who watches TV these days knows about the world-historical change that's on the way. Those who are optimistic about the change focus quite narrowly on the remarkably counterintuitive position that once we all own expensive office machines, then culture will become radically decentralized and the nightmare of the mass society, along with the age-old curse of elitism, will be ended for good.

But those of us who are concerned about the concentration of the media see the big change as essentially a negative one: the sky really is falling, civilization is wandering into a cultural catastrophe. Partially, of course, this is a predictable end-of-the-century sentiment, common to every year cursed with a nine as its third digit. But it's also a very real constellation of fears. We're "dumbing down." We've become incapable of judging. And nothing brings it home more concretely than the rise of culture trust, the group of media-moguls like Time Warner, Geffen, Disney, and Westinghouse who have fashioned a monopoly from American tastes. In formal terms what's happened looks like an almost literal realization of C. Wright Mills' classic definition of a mass society: ever fewer voices talking to an ever larger and an ever more passive audience.

Both doomsayers and cyberecstatics are talking about the same larger phenomenon, of which the rise of the "culture trust" is a central element. The defining fact of American life in the 1990s is its reorganization around the needs of the corporations, not just that we all work for them, and not just culturally, and not just in the sense that the only redemption anyone's hoping for is supposed to come through personal computers. The world of business, it seems, is becoming the world, period. The market is politics, the office is society, the brand is equivalent to human identity. *Fast Company*, one of the most prominent magazine start-ups of recent years, calls this "the business revolution" and trumpets itself as the "handbook." According to *Fast Company*, business culture is replacing civil society. "Work is personal" and "Computing is social" are points one and two in its manifesto for the corporate revolution. In one issue it proclaimed that the division of American business leaders into "cyber-libertarians" and "techno-communitarians" is "the *real* election," far overshadowing the obsolete battlings of Democrats and Republicans. If there's going to be any social justice in the world, the magazine argues, it will be because the market has decreed that there be social justice. One of the magazine's writers takes the argument all the way: "Corporations have become the dominant institution of our time," he writes, "occupying the position of the church of the Middle Ages and the nation-state of the past two centuries." A similar note is sounded in a recent *Newsday* article discussing the dramatic rise in popularity of management books: "The line between business and life are blurring a bit and work issues are becoming a 24-hour-a-day concern."[1]

The words and images that describe what many of us believe to be happening are surprisingly easy to summon. It's going to be the triumph of gray, of hierarchy, of homogeneity, of spirit-killing order. Right? We're all going to be robots—automaton organization men. We'll have to listen to Muzak all the time. It's going to be like *1984*, the most abused source of metaphors in metaphor history. It's going to be corporate feudalism like in *Rollerball* or one of those dystopic Schwarzenegger films. Right?

Wrong. The corporate takeover of life *is* coming; in fact, it's already happened. But what makes the culture of the businessman's republic so interesting is not that it demands order, conformity, gray clothes, and Muzak, but that it presents itself as an *opponent* to those very conceptions of corporate life. Those who speak for the new order aren't puritanical; they're hip; they're fully tuned in to youth culture; they listen to alternative rock while they work; they fantasize about smashing convention. Business theory today is about revolution, not about stasis or hierarchy; it's about liberation, not order. Business is "fast companies" questioning everything from job duties to pay scales to office furniture. Business is Sony Wonder, the brand-based amusement park at Madison and 54th Street. Business is "thinking outside the box," as anyone who's flipped through the latest management best-sellers must be tired of hearing. Business is tattooed executives snowboarding down K2 or parachuting in hurricane weather or riding mountain bikes in tornadoes or kayaking down lava flows or running shrieking down the halls of the great bureaucracies overturning desks and throwing paper. Business is adman Jay Chiat snipping off his clients' ties and "squash[ing] conventionality like ripe fruit"; it's Wieden and Kennedy, the ad agency that boasts of being organized after "a slime mold."

All this makes for a very peculiar national culture, one marked by a strange coexistence of, on the one hand, extreme political apathy and, on the other, extreme commercial extremism. Politically speaking, dissent against the market order has never been more negligible. In terms of our presidential candidates and the people who make up Congress, we are living in a time of greater consensus and conformity than the fifties. But take a look at our advertising. Mainstream commercial America is in love with revolution and alternative everything to a degree not even attained in the sixties. Even the word "extreme" itself is virtually everywhere, from Taco Bell's "extreme combos" to Boston Market's "extreme carvers" to Pontiac commercials in which the company announces that it is "taking it to the extreme." Not only can the center not hold, the center ceased to hold about thirty years ago. And nobody cares. Certainly the traditional guardians of order don't care, and certainly the business community doesn't care.

Hip is how business understands itself today. If we're ever going to challenge the power of the culture trust, the first thing we're going to have to do is understand that capitalism is different now, especially in the media and advertising industries. And if you think that the problem with capitalism is that it forces people to conform or to march in lockstep restrain their appetites or something like that, then I've got news for you: you don't have a problem with capitalism. You're going to do just fine in the corporate revolution.

If you talk about culture in the businessman's republic, sooner or later you have to talk about advertising. For all its recent complaints about difficult demographics and the demise of broadcasting, advertising remains the central ideological apparatus of the new capitalism. Advertising is the market's subsidizing mechanism, the free-enterprise version of the National Endowment for the Arts, the device through which any cultural enterprise succeeds or fails. Advertising is also the public face of capitalism, the device through which what Jackson Lears calls the "fables of abundance" are transmitted and elaborated; the language of the nation's management dreams and carnival fantasies. The people who make advertising are, in a very real sense, the ideologues of the corporate revolution: they are architects of dissatisfaction and of perpetual obsolescence. They are corporate Jacobins, businessmen who imagine the cultural slate wiped clean, with all nonbrand-oriented traditions and customs out the window forever. As *Fortune* magazine insisted back in 1951, the market is a place of permanent revolution, to an extent that Trotsky could never have imagined, and advertising executives are its permanent vanguard.

And though it is fun, and even vaguely "empowering," (to use the catch-all adjective of the businessman's republic) to talk about how oppressive and conformist consumer society is, if you look closely, you will notice that advertising, that society's paramount expression, is not particularly utopian. To be sure, here and there you will in fact find representations of families whose happiness is consummated by products, but by and large, the work of the cutting-edge agencies is anti-utopian. Advertising, at least on its surface, does not regard the new world of total corporate control as a happy thing.

In fact, much of advertising today is not only anti-utopian; it's full-on critical. It speaks directly to the problems of media, power, and culture. It makes exemplary use of all those images to which I referred earlier: people in the workplace as robots, in uniform gray, trapped in boxlike elevators and cubicles, driven by sadistic bosses. I chose these images, in fact, precisely because of their familiarity through advertising. Advertising recognizes that consumer society hasn't given us the things it promised or solved the problems it was supposed to do: that consumerism is in fact a gigantic sham. It's lots of hard work for no reason. The rat race. The treadmill. The office as hell.

Call this species of advertising "liberation marketing" (to borrow a phrase from Tom Peters). It knows that the culture trust exists, and it knows that business has conquered the world. And it offers in response not just soaps that get your whites whiter, but soaps that liberate you, soda pops that are emblems of individualism, radios of resistance, carnivalesque cars, and counterhegemonic hamburgers. Liberation marketing takes the old mass culture critique—consumerism as conformity—fully into account, acknowledges it, addresses it, and solves it. Liberation marketing imagines consumers breaking free from the old enforcers of order, tearing loose from the shackles with which capitalism has bound us, escaping the routine of bureaucracy and hierarchy, getting in touch with our true selves, and finally, finding authenticity, that holiest of consumer grails.

Liberation marketing can trace its roots back to the early 1960s, but its most important modern exposition was the famous TV commercial that introduced the Macintosh back in 1984, in which herds of people in gray were freed from the iron grip of Big Brother's propaganda telescreens. The ad was remarkable not only for the way it was filmed and the place it was shown (the Super Bowl, of course), but for daring to accept, and even endorse, the darkest vision of consumer society. We are a nation of look-alike suckers, it told us, glued to the tube, fastening intently on the words of the Man. That is, until

Macintosh arrives. The commercial not only set the tone for future Macintosh advertising, but for the entire body of propaganda for the cyber-revolution which now deluges us every day: computers are liberating; they empower us; they let us mouth off at the Man. Not incidentally, the ad was made by Chiat/Day, the same people who told us how Reebok "lets U.B.U." and who sent a gang of latter-day merry pranksters around the country for Fruitopia.

That was in 1984. In France, Macintosh advertising was even more direct, announcing that "It was about time a capitalist led a revolution." Today, French advertising executive Jean-Marie Dru writes that Apple has secured its grip on the liberator image: "Apple is not simply a brand of technologically revolutionary products. It's an antiestablishment company." Ever since then, other computer brands have vied for Macintosh's enviable antiestablishment position, the most notable recent example being Packard Bell, whose commercials treat us to

The mass society critique from academia to advertising agency: "Today, modern man is safe. Insulated from the elements, we have climate control, home shopping, 500 channels..."

visions of modern consuming life that come straight out of *Metropolis*. But the approach is hardly limited to computer advertising, or even to the handful of hip ad agencies.

Nowadays, you'll even find liberation marketing in such odd places as ads for chewing gum. Doublemint, for example, abandoned its happy jingle of many years to tantalize us with a vision of the workplace as white-collar sweatshop and their own product as a glimmer of child-like innocence that can be enjoyed surreptitiously anywhere.

Cars have always been escape machines, but by embracing the old mass society critique advertising is now able to depict much more convincingly what they're allowing us to escape from. Cars, like computers, free us from the grinding routine of office and commute. Cars offer us a serious attitude adjustment and let us color outside the lines. Here are highlights from three of my favorite auto commercials.

"...Are you really free? Are you really free? Are you really really really free?" (Volkswagen)

That old time anomie: "I've got gigabytes, I've got megabytes.
I'm voice-mailed, I'm e-mailed...I surf the net. I'm on the web. I am cyberman.
So how come I feel so out of touch?"

First, Volkswagen, which is as straightforward an indictment of mass
society as anything you'll find in the works of Hannah Arendt, and
as evocative a celebration of counterhegemonic cultural practice as
anything you'll read about in the works of John Fiske. Each install-
ment in the "Drivers Wanted" series identifies some aspect of consumer society which Volkswagen enables you to resist: fakeness,
overwork, boredom, compartmentalization, hierarchy. Especially
moving is the spot which describes the soulless glass-and-steel office
blocks, in which you are imprisoned.

One of the curious subtexts of this species of advertising, of which
the Volkswagen spots are such a wonderful example, is the way these
commercials mirror contemporary management philosophy, specifi-
cally those philosophies favored by the sponsor, the advertising
agency, or the target audience. This is done explicitly in another
French Macintosh ad, which Dru narrates for us in his recent book:

Ah, freedom. (Volkswagen)

...a rich Italian businessman gives his son a resolute speech on the virtues of being authoritarian with his employees. He explains that the workers are there to carry out orders and not to think. Otherwise, they'd want to change things, and this does not l e within the scope of their abilities. The voice-over of the ad concludes: "There are different ways of running a company. Here's one." The Apple logo appears on the screen. The voice-over continues: "Luckily, there are others."[2]

Volkswagen, of course, has been an anti-establishment brand since the late 1950s, and the "Drivers Wanted" commercials, whose victim-heroes are always identifiably good citizens of the businessman's republic, seemed to be pitched to the sort of people who write glowing letters to the editors of *Fast Company*. The slogan seems to be a way of saying that, on the road of life, there are entrepreneurs and then there are hapless organization drones.

Saab commercials do the same thing, just a little more upscale. One spot in particular imagines its clearly upper-middle-class protagonist rising up against the various social conventions that bind him: He will grow his hair however he wants; he will do whatever he feels like doing with his time; he will disregard the ordinary politenesses of genteel party-talk. He will find his own road. There's even a golden moment when he shocks the bourgeoisie.

The ways of the stodgy corporation are strictly for the birds, and no one knows it better than the organization man himself. The cartoon animation in this spot is also significant: being yourself, speaking

He's gone and offended the stuffy old bourgeoisie!: "When people ask for your honest opinion, you could give it to them." (Saab)

honestly—these are the dearest dreams of lifelong corporatrons, but they are only dreams, and must be rendered as cartoons.

Contemporary youth culture is, of course, the native tongue of liberation marketing, but it will also scour history for emblems of hip that are long dead, as in, of course, the Gap ads featuring Chet Baker, Monty Clift, and so on. Since the Beats are, apart from modern art, just about the earliest glimmering of the rebellion-through-style against mass society that defines liberation marketing, they and their works make up the revered canon of contemporary advertising. In one Volvo commercial, the only spoken words are lines from *On The Road,* the ultimate expression of this theme of car culture versus consumer culture.

It's significant that the people in this spot are visibly middle-aged. Anybody can read Kerouac; in fact, almost everybody still does. But it's important to Volvo that we understand that these are original beats, not some latter-day fakers, that they are true to the spirit of

"You could go off an write that novel. Climb that mountain. Buy those shoes.
You could fly in the face of convention." (Saab)

Kerouac, not just the image. This is established in a longer version of the commercial that shows the book's cover, which identifiably dates from the fifties. In the campaign's print ad the book is further detailed: "Always the romantic, John

remembered to bring *On The Road*. Not one of those new printings he'd seen in the bookstore at the mall, but the original one that he had stored away in the attic." Even advertising is down on mall culture! Find the authentic item in an attic somewhere, and hang it from the rear-view mirror in your Volvo.

Here's the Kerouac passage that is read in the commercial: "the only people for me are the mad ones, the ones who are mad to live, mad to talk, mad to be saved, desirous of everything at the same time, the ones who never yawn or say a commonplace thing." It's a virtual

Volvo drivers were *there,* man!

declaration of postmodern consumer desire: the hunger to consume everything at once; to defy the commonplace stuff that other people consume or that we consumed yesterday; to be "mad" rather than logocentric. It's a line that could be applied to virtually any product; a line that every copywriter should paste above his door; a line that belongs in the *Norton Anthology* of great consumer fantasies.

When I say that this is an age of conformity on a level that far exceeds that of the 1950s, I'm not saying that there is no cultural dissidence in America. In fact, we have a superabundance of it. Even oldsters who drive the sensible Volvo recognize that the "only ones" are the "mad ones," not the gray flannels, not the organization men, but the people whose craving for authenticity and escape can never be assuaged. And look around at media other than advertising: we are an immensely cynical people when it comes to the culture trust. Media workers, their bosses, and suits in general are stereotypical villains to the point of cliché in contemporary mass culture. Nobody except Newt Gingrich likes Rupert Murdoch. Thanks to Vance Packard and William Whyte, we all know about planned obsolescence. According to a study done by Ogilvy & Mather (and reported by James Twitchell in *Adcult USA*),[3] 62 percent of us believe in subliminal ads, believe that advertising works through some sort of Cold-War-style conspiracy of subconscious manipulation. We are willing to believe the worst, even when it's not true. We know bad things are happening to our political and social universe; we know that business is colonizing ever larger chunks of American culture; we know

that the boss believes "Work is personal" and "Computing is social," even if we don't; and we know that advertising tells lies. We are all sick to death of the consumer culture. We know it's a fraud; we know it's a fake; we know it's all wrong. We all want to resist conformity. We all want to be our own dog.

And yet we do nothing. Congress just gave away another enormous chunk of the broadcast spectrum with only a whisper of dissent.

I want to suggest that our apathy has a very specific relationship to liberation marketing. The market works not only to redefine dissent, but to occupy the niche that dissident voices used to occupy in the American cultural spectrum. Among people who write critically about advertising, there's always been a sense that advertising and politics are somehow negatively connected; that there's an inverse relationship between the prevalence of advertising and America's political apathy. Even Marshall McLuhan pointed this out back in 1947, telling a story of how

> an American army officer wrote for *Printer's Ink* from Italy. He noted with misgiving that Italians could tell you the names of cabinet ministers but not the names of commodities preferred by Italian celebrities. Furthermore, the wall space of Italian cities was given over to political rather than commercial slogans. Finally, he predicted that there was small hope that Italians would ever achieve any sort of domestic prosperity or calm until they began to worry about the rival claims of cornflakes or cigarettes rather than the capacities of public men. In fact, he went so far as to say that democratic freedom very largely consists in ignoring politics and worrying about the means of defeating underarm odor, scaly scalp, hairy legs, dull complexion, unruly hair, borderline anaemia, athlete's foot, and sluggish bowels....[4]

The point that I'm trying to make is not that advertising somehow tricks us into ignoring our problems, but that the culture of consumerism has undergone an enormous change. Dissidence has become a function of the marketplace; existential nausea is becoming just as powerful an element of brand loyalty as the twelve ways in which Wonder-bread built strong bodies ever were. When we talk about nonconformity, we're increasingly talking about those particularly outspoken entrepreneurs who are detailed in *Wired* magazine; when we talk about breaking the rules, we're talking about the people who stay up all night to work at their firm but listen to alternative rock while doing so. This is a point that Dru makes explicitiy: every brand must have an identity, and the most effective identities are found when a brand takes on the trappings of a movement for social justice. Writes Dru:

> The great brands of this end of the century are those that have succeeded in conveying their vision by questioning certain conventions, whether it's Apple's humanist vision, which reverses the relationship between people and machines; Benetton's libertarian vision, which overthrows communication conventions; Microsoft's progressive vision, which topples bureaucratic barriers; or Virgin's anticonformist vision, which rebels against the powers that be.[4]

The Body Shop owns compassion, Nike spirituality, Pepsi and MTV youthful rebellion.

With its constant talk of liberation, of radical new officing techniques, the advertising industry is filling a very specific niche in the cultural spectrum of the businessman's republic. As business replaces civil society, advertising is taking over the cultural functions that used to be filled by the left. Dreaming of a better world is now the work of business. We used to have movements for change; now we have products. As American politics become ever more deaf to the idea that the market might not be the best solution for every social problem, the market, bless its invisible heart, is seeing to it that the duties of the left do not go unfilled.

According to the attack on advertising made by the critics of mass society, Madison Avenue was the nerve-center of conformist evil. But while the mass society critique has largely disappeared from the academia where it was first spawned, it has been taken up by none other than its old arch-villain, Madison Avenue, and transformed into a sort of American permacritique. It never goes away, no matter how it is refuted, and no matter how out-of-date its economic appraisal becomes. Advertising will go on telling us that the problem with society is conformity, and that the answer is carnival, as long as there remains a discretionary dollar in the last teenager's allowance. If our famously-fragmented society has anything approaching a master narrative, it's more of a master conflict, like during the Cold War: now we are in constant struggle not with the Communists, but with the puritanical, spirit-crushing, fakeness-pushing power of consumer society; and we resist by dancing, or by watching Madonna videos, or by

"…Hey. That's the stuff we're made of." (Pizza Hut)

consorting with more authentic people thanks to our Sport-Utility vehicle, or by celebrating the consumers who do these things.

Daniel Bell once declared that the conflict between the enforced efficiency of the workplace and the hedonistic blow-off of our leisure time was one of capitalism's most devastating "cultural contradictions." But now we know better: the market solves for the market's problems, at least superficially. Criticism of capitalism has become, in a very strange way, capitalism's lifeblood. It's a closed ideological system, within which (at least symbolically) criticism can be addressed and resolved.

If the problems of capitalism are things like lack of authenticity and soul-deadening conformity, well, then capitalism can solve its own problems very effectively, and it has been solving them since the 1960s. If, on the other hand, your idea of capitalism's problems swings more heavily towards social problems like labor practices and improverishment and union-busting, then you're talking about something else altogether. This is a critique that advertising will never embrace. No matter how hard up Reebok gets, it will never use the fact of Nike's Indonesian sweatshops to improve its position; no, it'll just keep talking about how its shoes let U. B. U. Like about thirty other products do.

Not that advertising doesn't try to address concrete social problems. In fact there have been a spate of ads lately in which various get-rich-quick schemes are sold as solutions to unemployment.

Perhaps most egregious is the Pizza Hut commercial that addresses the increasingly undeniable incidence of—gasp—labor discord. Entitled (believe it or not) "Bad Break," the ad juxtaposes a group of generically angry workers stomping around outside a factory with a group of generically concerned executives. As tension mounts, a truck pulls up and delivers pizza to the striking workers, who drop their picket signs and smile gratefully at the white-collar figures up above. And so, thanks to the management team, a century of labor struggle has been swept away.

So we're back to where we started: the world of business is the world, period. There's nothing outside of it; it's a closed universe. Get as mad as you want, just be sure the pizza trucks are standing by.

Notes

1   John Mahoney, an editor at Times Business publishers, quoted in *Newsday*, Sept. 22, 1996, p. F9.

2   Jean-Marie Dru, *Disruption: Overturning Conventions and Shaking Up the Marketplace* (New York: John Wiley, 1996), p. 106.

3   NY: Columbia University Press, 1996, p. 116.

4   Marshall McLuhan, "American Advertising," in Rosenberg and White, *Mass Culture*, 1957, (NY: The Free Press of Glencoe, 1957) 435.

5   Dru, p. 214.

About the Contributors

Patricia Aufderheide is an associate professor in the Department of Communication at American University.

Erik Barnouw is the author of *A History of Broadcasting in the United States* (Oxford University Press), *Tube of Plenty* (Oxford University Press), and many other books.

Richard M. Cohen is the former senior producer of the *CBS Evening News*.

Thomas C. Frank is the editor-in-chief of *The Baffler*. He is the author of *The Conquest of Cool* (University of Chicago Press) and coeditor of *Commodify Your Dissent* (W. W. Norton).

Todd Gitlin teaches in the Department of Culture and Communication at New York University. He is the author of *The Sixties* and, most recently, of *The Twilight of Common Dreams* (Metropolitan Books).

David Lieberman is the media analyst at *USA Today*.

Mark Crispin Miller, chairman of the Writing Seminars at Johns Hopkins University, is the author of *Boxed In* (Northwestern University Press) and a forthcoming study of U.S. propaganda, *Mad Scientists* (W. W. Norton).

Gene Roberts is the managing editor of the *New York Times*.

Thomas Schatz teaches in the Department of Radio/TV/Film at the University of Texas, Austin. He is the author of *The Genius of the System* (Metropolitan Books).